The Old Farmer's Almanac Home Library

BEST HOME
BAKING

Irresistible Recipes from
America's Blue Ribbon Bakers

Polly Bannister

AND THE EDITORS OF
The Old Farmer's Almanac

This book is dedicated to my mother, Patricia Holmes Bannister, an enthusiastic and creative cook. Although it has been many, many years since she prepared those delicious (and countless) meals for our family of eight, I continue to feel thankful to her for a lifetime of nourishment.
— P.B.

OLD FARMER'S ALMANAC HOME LIBRARY
Series Editor: Sarah Elder Hale
Consulting Editor: Susan Peery
Copy Editor: Barbara Jatkola
Art Director: Karen Savary
Layout: Sheryl Fletcher
Cover Illustration: Sara Love
Illustrations, pp. 15, 33, 43, 53, 65, 77, 91, 95, 109, 121, 133: Karen Savary

LIBRARY OF CONGRESS CATALOGING-IN-PUBLICATION DATA
Bannister, Polly.
Best home baking : irresistible recipes from America's
Blue Ribbon bakers / Polly Bannister and the editors of the
Old farmer's almanac. p. cm. — (Old farmer's almanac
home library) Includes index.
ISBN 0-7370-0025-2
1. Baking. 2. Festivals — United States. 3. Fairs —
United States. I. Old farmer's almanac. II. Title. III. Series
TX763.B34   1998
641.8 ' 15 — dc21 98-17187 CIP

Distributed in the book trade by Time-Life Books, Inc.

TIME-LIFE BOOKS IS A DIVISION OF TIME LIFE INC.

TIME-LIFE CUSTOM PUBLISHING
Vice President and Publisher: Terry Newell
Vice President of Sales and Marketing: Neil Levin
Director of Acquisitions: Jennifer Pearce
Director of Special Markets: Liz Ziehl
Director of Design: Christopher Register
Project Manager: Linda Bellamy

TIME-LIFE is a trademark of Time Warner Inc. U.S.A.

Contents

Chapter 1 **Yeast Breads**   15

Honey Whole-Wheat Bread • White Bread • Corn-
meal Yeast Rolls • Old-Fashioned Potato Bread •
Wheat Germ Herb Bread • Onion Lovers' Bread
• Greek Anise Bread • Golden Pumpkin Raisin Bread
• Sourdough Onion-Potato Rye Bread with Caraway
• Rye Bread • Dinner Rolls • Honey Oatmeal Bread •
Orange Bread

*How Yeast Works • The Mystery of Gluten • Baking
with Rye Flour*

Foreword

*T*HE OLD FARMER'S ALMANAC, NOW IN ITS THIRD CENTURY OF publication, has always concerned itself with the basics of daily life, from the predictable movements of the sun, the moon, and other heavenly bodies to the weather (less predictable), household advice, gardening, and food. To be honest, though, it's only in the past half century or so that food and recipes have played a big role.

The founder of the Almanac and its editor for the first 54 years, Robert B. Thomas (1766–1846), left us only slight evidence of his culinary tastes. For instance, he recommended in his 1834 Almanac what he considered a superior way of roasting potatoes in the fireplace. Thomas said to wrap the potatoes individually in several layers of paper, soak them in water, and then roast them in hot ashes until the paper dried out and the potatoes were done. Although Thomas was a contemporary of the French gastronome Anthelme Brillat-Savarin, we are quite confident that they never met. If they had, we venture that they would have jousted over Brillat-Savarin's statement, "The discovery of a new dish does more for human happiness than the discovery of a new star." Thomas, who had studied almanac-making at a special school in Boston and who made all his own astronomical calculations, strikes us as someone who would have cast his lot with the new star.

We still have reams of astronomical calculations in *The Old Farmer's Almanac,* but over the years food and cooking have grown in importance. In fact, we have recently started several other annual publications, including *The Good Cook's Companion, Guide to Summer's Best Recipes,* and *Traditional Holiday Recipes,* all of which are devoted to the delicious subject of food. The recipe contest in the Almanac itself attracts hundreds of entries every year from the United States and Canada. The editorial staff evaluates and tests all the recipes — and that includes tasting them.

9

Devouring, in some cases. (A tough job, you might be thinking.) We want every recipe to be accurate in its measurements and methods, and easy enough for anyone with modest experience to make. Most of all, we want the food to look good and taste good.

You can imagine how happy we were to hear about Polly Bannister's new book, *Best Home Baking:* more recipe tasting at our offices in Dublin, New Hampshire! Best of all, this book is devoted to baking, my favorite form of cookery. Both the process and the product are satisfying, and the smells and tastes of homemade baked goods linger in our memories, forever linked with that special birthday party, the memorable potluck supper where everyone brought dessert (this really happened!), and the romantic dinner you cooked for someone you love.

As far as food goes, we've come a long way from Robert B. Thomas's "recipe" for fireplace potatoes. On the other hand, with a little salt, pepper, and butter, they might be quite good.

SUSAN PEERY
Managing Editor
The Old Farmer's Almanac
Dublin, New Hampshire

Introduction

*I*N YOUR HANDS IS A BOOK THAT IS A SEQUEL OF SORTS. *Best Home Baking* comes after my first book, *Blue Ribbon Recipes,* which evolved from my research on America's fairs and festivals for an article in *The Old Farmer's Almanac.* In the process of gathering recipes for two "blue ribbon" books, I have come to rely on the culinary arts directors, superintendents, and home arts administrators of fairs large and small across the country. These are the people who responded enthusiastically to my initial call. They care deeply about good homemade food and the cooks who bring their dishes to fairs. They do everything from choosing judges to setting up tables, awarding ribbons, organizing volunteers, and speaking at schools and church groups to encourage youngsters to compete at fairs. They lament only one thing — that they never have a minute to enjoy the festivities. (I learned early on *not* to call during fair time!)

The culinary chairmen and chairwomen also are the liaisons between local cooks and corporate sponsors such as Softasilk, Land O' Lakes, Nestlé, Crisco, and Archway. And, most important for me, they are the connections between an editor and the recipes. Over the past five years, they have mailed and faxed me hundreds of recipes, often with handwritten notes: "Yummy! Wins every year" or "This cake tasted as good as it looked." Sometimes I learn about the cook: "She has exhibited every year for the past 25" or "Her mom won with this same recipe years ago." Without the generosity of these fair folks, I could not have uncovered the great recipes you'll find here.

For example, when I called Cathy Poluzzi, culinary chairwoman of the Dutchess County Fair in Rhinebeck, New York, she gave me more than 50 recipes from which to choose. When we tried Sima's Yummy Rugelach (page 140) and selected it for this book, Cathy was overjoyed. She said, "You should talk to Sima Firine. She is nearly 90 and came to America from Russia." I called, and Sima told me that the recipe was her mother's, brought from Russia when the family was smuggled out in 1922.

At the Iowa State Fair (one of the country's oldest and largest), Arlette Hollister handpicked some favorites from the 7,000 food entries they receive each year, and we snatched up Ann McWilliam's Empire Biscuits (page 135). Our recipe tester agrees with Arlette — you'll not find a better shortbread recipe anywhere.

Speaking of our recipe tester, she is as much a contributor to this book as the fair directors and cooks. Kate Thomas of Fitzwilliam, New Hampshire, is one of the finest bakers we know. She has never officially studied cooking. In fact, she has a degree in Russian language and literature from Radcliffe. "My interest in baking began when I was ten," she says, "and was assigned bread making as a family chore. I think a part of why I cook so much is that I am a fussy eater and I know just what I want." Kate's pickiness is our gain. She tested for *Blue Ribbon Recipes,* and her comments were always precise and interesting.

Kate spent the better part of three months in her kitchen baking. She fed family, friends, and neighbors, making note of their opinions. Her best critics were husband Ben and sons Gareth and Gawain. Kate told me, "When the boys begged me to repeat a recipe, as in the case of Gawain's favorite, Coconut Cake (page 78), I knew we had a winner." When I called Kate to confer, I often heard the clanging of pots being washed in the background. She'd say, "Thank goodness for Ben; he does most of the cleanup." Ben had another important job — dropping off goodies at our office in Dublin on his way to his carpentry job. We'd see him coming and get a fresh pot of coffee going.

We hope you'll enjoy these delicious recipes as much as we have.

Judging Scorecards

WE ALL REALIZE THAT TASTE IS SUBJECTIVE, AND FOR THIS reason judging food is really quite difficult. Quantifying expressions such as "Yummy" and "Mmmmm," accompanied by vigorous head nodding, makes the job of a food judge a real challenge. After years of experience, contest managers have developed rating systems that assign point values to important characteristics of dishes in competition. Point values may vary at each fair, but in general you'll find that flavor and appearance account for most of the score. To give you an idea of what judges look for in baked goods, here are some sample scorecards from the Ozark Empire Fair in Springfield, Missouri.

Yeast Breads

Flavor: Blend of well-baked ingredients, free from sourness	30
Texture: Tender, free from dryness or doughiness	25
Grain: Fine cells, evenly distributed	15
Crust: Uniform browning, free from cracks and bulges	15
Color: Characteristic of ingredients used, free from dark streaks	15

Quick Breads

Shape, Color, Volume: Well proportioned; evenly rounded or flat top depending on type of bread; uniformly brown; light weight in proportion to size   30

Crumb: Well raised and equally light throughout; moist, elastic, tender; medium-fine, round, even cells; flaky lightness; no tunnels; not dry or soggy; nuts and fruit evenly distributed   30

Flavor: Blended flavor of well-baked ingredients; free from flavor of fat, baking powder, or salt   30

Crust: Crisp, usually rough surface; tender, thin, no cracks   10

Cakes

Flavor: Delicate and pleasing, well blended   35

Texture: Cakes with butter/shortening should be tender, moist, light, and have fine even cells; cakes without fat should be tender, feathery, resilient, and have fine even cells   35

Appearance: *Shape:* straight sides, slightly rounded top; *crust:* smooth, uniform color, not cracked or sticky; *frosting:* glossy, smooth, not too thick, suitable for cake; *filling:* minimum one-quarter inch, fluffy, good flavor, suitable for cake   30

Pies

Crust: Texture flaky and tender; flavor agreeable, no strong taste of fat or salt   40

Filling: Characteristic flavor, not over- or undersweetened or spiced; *consistency:* custards thoroughly cooked, thick, and smooth, or fruit thick, firm, yet tender, neither too juicy nor too dry; meringue light, tender, slightly sweet, at least one-half inch thick, no shrinking or weeping   40

Appearance: Color and shape   20

Cookies

Flavor: Well blended, natural flavor of ingredients   50

Texture: Tender, small even cells, not crumbly or hard, consistent with type of cookie; thin cookie crisp; drop cookie soft; bar cookie moist   30

Appearance: Shape regular, color uniform, free from darkened edges   20

Chapter 1

Yeast Breads

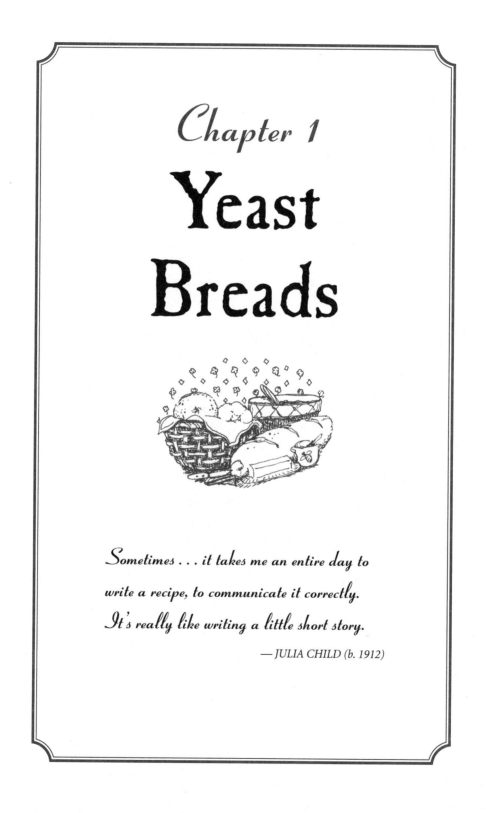

Sometimes . . . it takes me an entire day to write a recipe, to communicate it correctly. It's really like writing a little short story.

—JULIA CHILD (b. 1912)

Honey Whole-Wheat Bread

2 loaves

The cook won "Best of Show" for this recipe, which the judges said looked as good as it tasted. Our recipe tester agreed wholeheartedly, saying that this bread has become a family favorite. For a tasty variation, try adding ¼ cup flaxseeds and ¼ cup sesame seeds.

4 cups whole-wheat flour, divided	3 cups water
½ cup nonfat powdered milk	½ cup honey
1 tablespoon salt	2 tablespoons vegetable oil
2 packages (2 tablespoons) dry yeast	3½ to 4 cups white flour cornmeal

In a large mixer bowl, combine 3 cups of the whole-wheat flour, powdered milk, salt, and yeast. Mix well. Heat the water, honey, and vegetable oil until warm (115° to 120° F). Add the warm liquid to the dry ingredients and beat on low for 30 seconds, scraping the bowl constantly. Beat on medium for 3 minutes more. By hand, stir in the remaining 1 cup whole-wheat flour and enough of the white flour to make a moderately stiff dough. Turn out onto a floured surface and knead for about 5 minutes. Place in a greased bowl, cover, and let rise until doubled in bulk, 45 to 60 minutes.

Punch the dough down. Divide in half, cover, and let rest for 10 minutes. Grease two 9×5-inch pans and sprinkle with cornmeal. Shape the dough into 2 loaves and place in the pans. Cover and let rise until doubled in bulk, about 30 to 45 minutes.

Preheat the oven to 375° F. Bake for 30 to 35 minutes. Cool on wire racks for 10 minutes before removing from the pans.

Reverend Nancy S. Donnelly, Glen Gardner, New Jersey
Flemington Agricultural Fair, Flemington, New Jersey

White Bread

2 loaves

This is an excellent recipe for basic white bread. Everyone loves it straight out of the oven.

2 packages (2 tablespoons)
  dry yeast
2¼ cups warm water, divided
3 tablespoons sugar
1 tablespoon salt

2 tablespoons shortening
  or butter
6 to 7 cups flour, divided
melted butter

In a large bowl, dissolve the yeast in ½ cup of the warm water. Stir in the remaining 1¾ cups water, sugar, salt, shortening or butter, and 3½ cups of the flour. Beat until smooth. (The electric mixer is a real help here.) Stir in enough of the remaining flour to make the dough easy to handle. Turn the dough out onto a lightly floured surface and knead until light and elastic. Place in a greased bowl, cover, and let rise until doubled in bulk, about 1 hour.

Punch the dough down and divide it in half. Shape into 2 loaves and place in greased loaf pans (either 9×5-inch or 8½×4½-inch). Brush lightly with melted butter, cover, and let rise until doubled in bulk, about 1 hour.

Preheat the oven to 425° F and bake for 25 to 30 minutes, or until the loaves are golden brown and sound hollow when tapped. Remove from the pans, brush the tops with more melted butter, and cool on wire racks.

Cathy Stark, Stanfordville, New York
Dutchess County Fair, Rhinebeck, New York

Blue Ribbon Tip

HOW YEAST WORKS

Fair-going cooks who bake their bread on summer days recognize that dough can rise too fast during hot weather, resulting in big air bubbles in the dough. They must find a cooler place for their bread to rise. Bread that rises more slowly will be more finely textured and often better tasting than bread that has been rushed along.

Yeast differs from other leavening agents in that it is actually alive. Yeasts are tiny organisms that occur naturally; their spores are floating in the air we breathe. Yeast can be captured from the wild and cultivated simply by exposing flour and water to the air. This is the source of the well-known sourdough starters. Obviously, doing this could result in catching the spores of less desirable strains of yeast, not to mention the spores of molds. Hence the development of dry yeast. In this form, we can think of yeast as a seed. When moisture and warmth awaken it from its dormant state, it starts to digest, to excrete carbon dioxide, and to reproduce. It finds plenty of nutrients in the flour present in the dough. Many recipes jump-start the yeast by mixing it with a little sugar water before combining it with other ingredients, but this is not essential.

When the yeast excretes carbon dioxide, the bubbles of carbon dioxide are what puff the bread up to make it rise. However, in an environment containing too much carbon dioxide, the yeast shuts down. That is why we punch the dough down periodically — to release the carbon dioxide so that the yeast can resume its process of digestion, excretion, and reproduction. Yeast reproduces very fast, so each rising will take less time than the previous one because a larger number of organisms are taking part. When the bread is baked, the yeast is killed.

Cornmeal Yeast Rolls

1 dozen rolls

The cook won first prize with these rolls when she was a student at Byron Middle School. They are tasty and light like a white roll, but they have some whole grain for extra flavor. A first-rate recipe.

1¼ cups cornmeal
1 cup boiling water
1 package (1 tablespoon) dry yeast
½ cup warm water
¾ cup scalded milk, cooled to
   lukewarm

½ cup (1 stick) butter or
   margarine, melted
⅓ cup sugar
2 egg yolks, slightly beaten
2 teaspoons salt
4 to 5 cups flour

Combine the cornmeal and boiling water in a large bowl. Stir well and let stand for about 10 minutes. In a medium-size bowl, dissolve the yeast in the warm water. Let stand for 5 minutes. Add the milk, butter, sugar, egg yolks, and salt; blend well. Gradually add the yeast mixture to the cornmeal mixture, stirring well. Gradually add enough flour to make a soft dough. Turn the dough out onto a lightly floured surface and knead until smooth and elastic, about 5 minutes. Place in a greased bowl, turning to grease the top. Cover and let rise in a warm place (85° F) for 1 hour, or until doubled in bulk.

Punch the dough down and shape into 12 round rolls. Place on a greased baking sheet, cover, and let rise until doubled in bulk, about 30 to 45 minutes. Preheat the oven to 425° F. Bake for 20 minutes, or until golden brown. Serve warm.

Amber Brook, Byron, Georgia
Georgia National Fair, Perry, Georgia

Old-Fashioned Potato Bread

2 loaves

Here is what our recipe tester had to say about this recipe: "Yummy, beautiful, a keeper!"

2 cups warm water
2 packages (2 tablespoons)
    dry yeast
½ cup sugar
1 tablespoon salt
1 cup warm mashed potatoes
    (about 2 medium-size potatoes)

½ cup (1 stick) butter or
    margarine, softened
2 eggs
7½ cups flour, divided
3 tablespoons butter or
    margarine, divided
flour for dusting (optional)

Put the warm water in a large mixer bowl. Sprinkle with the yeast and stir until dissolved. Add the sugar and salt; stir until dissolved. Add the mashed potatoes, softened butter, eggs, and 3½ cups of the flour. Beat on medium until smooth, about 2 minutes. Gradually add the remaining 4 cups flour, mixing with a wooden spoon or your hands until the dough is smooth and stiff enough to leave the sides of the bowl. (The dough will be soft.) Melt 1 tablespoon of the butter and spread it over the dough. Cover with a double thickness of aluminum foil or plastic wrap. Let rise in the refrigerator for about 2 hours, or until doubled in bulk. Punch the dough down. Cover and refrigerate overnight.

The next day, turn the dough out onto a lightly floured surface. Knead until smooth and elastic and blisters appear on the surface, about 10 minutes. Divide the dough in half and shape each half into a smooth ball about 6 inches in diameter. Place each in a lightly greased 9-inch round cake pan. Melt the remaining 2 tablespoons butter and brush over the dough. Cover with a kitchen towel and let rise in a warm place (85° F) until doubled in bulk, about 1½ to 2 hours.

Preheat the oven to 400° F. With a sharp knife, make 3 cuts crosswise in the surface of each loaf. Then make 3 cuts lengthwise to create a criss-cross pattern. Bake for 40 to 45 minutes, or until the loaves are well browned and sound hollow when tapped. Remove from the pans and cool on wire racks. If desired, dust the tops lightly with flour before serving.

Mrs. Cloyce Hollis, Belleville, Wisconsin
The Old Farmer's Almanac Recipe Contest, Dublin, New Hampshire

Wheat Germ Herb Bread

2 loaves

Mary Frances Scheetz lived in Canfield, Ohio, for 25 years before retiring to Florida. Before leaving her hometown, she won many blue ribbons for her breads. This herb-scented bread makes a delicious accompaniment to almost any meal. You might want to vary the herbs to complement your main dish: basil and oregano to go with Italian dishes, dill and rosemary with fish.

5½ to 6½ cups flour, divided
2 packages (2 tablespoons) dry yeast
1 teaspoon salt
⅓ cup sugar
1 teaspoon dried thyme leaves, crushed
1 teaspoon dried marjoram leaves, crushed
1½ cups milk
½ cup water
½ cup (1 stick) butter or margarine
2 whole eggs
1 egg, separated
1⅓ cups plus 1 tablespoon wheat germ, divided

In a large mixer bowl, combine 3 cups of the flour, yeast, salt, sugar, thyme, and marjoram; mix well. In a saucepan, heat the milk, water, and butter until warm (the butter does not have to melt). Add to the flour mixture along with the 2 whole eggs and 1 egg yolk. Beat for 3 minutes. Gradually stir in 1⅓ cups of the wheat germ and enough of the remaining flour to make a soft dough. Knead on a floured surface until smooth and elastic, about 10 minutes. Place in a greased bowl, turning to grease the top. Cover and let rise until doubled in bulk, about 1 hour.

Punch the dough down and divide into quarters. Form each part into a rope and twist 2 together to make a loaf. Fold the ends in and place in a greased loaf pan (either 9×5-inch or 8½×4½-inch). Repeat with the other 2 pieces of dough. Cover and let rise for 30 to 40 minutes.

Preheat the oven to 350° F. Lightly brush the dough with the egg white and sprinkle with the remaining 1 tablespoon wheat germ. Bake for 35 to 40 minutes. Loosely cover with aluminum foil for the last 5 to 10 minutes of baking. Remove from the pans and cool on wire racks.

Mary Frances Scheetz, Fort Myers, Florida
Canfield Fair, Canfield, Ohio

Onion Lovers' Bread

1 loaf

Although this is not a true sourdough bread, the tangy starter gives it a delicious zip. The starter needs to be made a day ahead. This recipe won "Best of Show," and with good reason — it is both gorgeous and delicious.

Starter
2 cups flour
2 tablespoons sugar
1 tablespoon malt vinegar
1 tablespoon salt
1½ cups lukewarm water

Bread
1 package (1 tablespoon) dry yeast
¾ cup warm water, divided
1 cup starter
½ cup olive oil
½ cup milk
2 tablespoons honey
1½ teaspoons salt
1 egg
4 to 5 cups flour, divided

Filling
¼ cup (½ stick) butter
1 cup minced onion
2 large cloves garlic, minced
¼ cup freshly grated Parmesan
   cheese
2 tablespoons poppy seeds
1 teaspoon paprika

1 egg beaten with 1 tablespoon
   water

To make the starter, combine all the ingredients thoroughly. The mixture will be thick. Cover and let sit at least 24 hours before using. After using, replenish by adding equal amounts of warm water and flour plus 1 teaspoon sugar.

To make the bread, in a large bowl dissolve the yeast in ¼ cup of the warm water. Let stand until dissolved. Stir in the starter, oil, milk, remaining ½ cup water, honey, salt, and egg. Add 2 cups of the flour and mix thoroughly. Knead in enough of the remaining flour, 1 cup at a time, to produce a smooth, not sticky, dough. Rub the top of the dough with oil, place in a bowl, cover, and let rise until doubled in bulk.

To make the filling, while the bread is rising, heat the butter in a skillet and sauté the onion and garlic lightly. Remove from the heat and stir in the Parmesan cheese, poppy seeds, and paprika. Cool.

When the dough has risen, punch it down and let it rest for 10 minutes. Roll out into an 18×12-inch rectangle and spread with the filling. Cut into 3 lengthwise strips. Carefully pinch together the edges of each strip to make 3 stuffed ropes of dough. On a greased baking sheet, loosely braid the ropes together and tuck the ends underneath. Cover and let rise for 30 to 40 minutes, or until doubled in bulk.

Preheat the oven to 375° F. Brush the dough with the egg-water mixture and bake for 35 to 40 minutes, or until the loaf is golden brown and sounds hollow when tapped. Cool on the baking sheet for 10 minutes, then transfer to a wire rack to cool completely.

Vickie Medlin, Dallas, Texas
State Fair of Texas, Dallas, Texas

Blue Ribbon Tip

THE MYSTERY OF GLUTEN

One of the mysteries of flour is its wonderful ability to form gluten. In the presence of water and agitation, two proteins present in flour join together to make long, stringy, elastic threads of gluten. This is what gives bread dough its wonderfully stretchy character. The five- to ten-minute kneading most bread recipes call for is essential to develop the gluten, and hence the elasticity of the dough. The dough's elastic quality lets it stretch as the yeast produces bubbles of carbon dioxide, and so the dough rises. Too much sugar or fat can retard the development of gluten and slow the rising of dough.

Greek Anise Bread

1 loaf

Here is another of Mary Frances Scheetz's blue ribbon winners.

1 package (1 tablespoon) active
   dry yeast
¼ cup warm water
⅓ cup sugar
¼ cup (½ stick) butter
½ teaspoon salt
½ cup milk, scalded
¼ teaspoon oil of anise

6 drops oil of cinnamon
3 cups flour (approximately),
   divided
1 egg
1 egg beaten with 1 tablespoon
   cold water
2 tablespoons sesame seeds

Soften the yeast in the water. Place the sugar, butter, and salt in a bowl and pour the hot milk over them. Stir until the butter melts. Cool to lukewarm. Stir in the oil of anise and oil of cinnamon. Add 1 cup of the flour. Mix well. Stir in the egg and softened yeast; beat well. Add enough of the remaining flour to make a soft dough. Turn out onto a lightly floured surface. Cover and let rest for 10 minutes.

Knead the dough until smooth and elastic, about 10 minutes. Place in a lightly oiled bowl, turning once to grease the surface. Cover and let rise until doubled in bulk, about 1¼ hours. Punch down and let rise again until almost doubled in bulk, about 1 hour.

Turn the dough out onto a floured surface and divide into 3 balls. Cover and let rest for 10 minutes. Roll each ball into a strand about 16 inches long, with tapered ends. Place the strands about 1 inch apart on a greased baking sheet. Braid loosely without stretching the dough, beginning in the middle and working toward either end. Pinch the ends together. Cover and let rise until doubled in bulk, about 40 minutes.

Preheat the oven to 375° F. Brush the dough with the egg-water mixture and sprinkle with the sesame seeds. Bake for 25 minutes, or until the loaf sounds hollow when tapped.

Mary Frances Scheetz, Fort Myers, Florida
Canfield Fair, Canfield, Ohio

Golden Pumpkin Raisin Bread

2 loaves

This sweet bread is sure to please.

2 packages (2 tablespoons) dry yeast	2 teaspoons salt
½ cup sugar	2 teaspoons ground cinnamon
⅔ cup warm water	1½ teaspoons ground ginger
1 can (16 ounces) solid-pack pumpkin	½ teaspoon ground nutmeg
	6¼ to 7¼ cups flour, divided
¼ cup vegetable oil	2 eggs
	1½ cups raisins

In a large bowl, sprinkle the yeast and sugar over the warm water; stir until dissolved. Add the pumpkin, oil, salt, cinnamon, ginger, nutmeg, and 1½ cups of the flour. Using a mixer on low speed, beat until well blended. Increase the mixer speed to medium and beat for 2 minutes more. Add the eggs and 1 cup flour; beat for 2 minutes. Stir in the raisins and enough of the remaining flour to make a moderately soft dough. Turn out onto a lightly floured surface. Knead until smooth and elastic, about 5 to 8 minutes. Place in a large greased bowl, turning the dough so that the top is greased. Cover with a kitchen towel and let rise in a warm place until doubled in bulk, about 1 hour. Note that because of the high sugar content, it is essential that the first rising be in a warm place; room temperature will not do. For the best results, put the bowl in a 125° F oven for 20 minutes to get things going.

Punch the dough down and divide it in half. Let rest for 10 minutes. Shape each half into a loaf. Place each loaf in a greased 9×5-inch pan. Cover and let rise until doubled in bulk, about 45 minutes.

Preheat the oven to 375° F. Bake for 35 to 40 minutes, or until the loaves are golden brown and sound hollow when tapped. Remove from the pans and cool on wire racks.

Stephanie Leach, Los Gatos, California
The Old Farmer's Almanac Recipe Contest, Dublin, New Hampshire

Sourdough Onion-Potato Rye Bread with Caraway

3 loaves

Paul was a member of the Poughkeepsie Police Department for 35 years, during which time he never baked. After retiring, he took an adult education course in bread making taught by a student at the Culinary Institute of America. He now makes bread for family celebrations, his local Catholic church, and, of course, the fair.

Making a real sourdough bread is a whole new adventure for many cooks. This recipe is fun to make, and even though it appears complicated, it really isn't. While making the starter (rye sour), you may feel like an alchemist, and the people eating the delicious, moist slices will surely think that you have been working magic.

Rye Sour
2½ cups rye flour, divided
⅓ teaspoon dry yeast
2½ cups warm water, divided
1 tablespoon caraway seeds,
    crushed or ground in a
    coffee grinder
½ medium-size onion, minced
1½ cups white flour, divided

Filling
½ medium-size onion, minced
2 teaspoons caraway seeds
2 teaspoons olive oil
dash of salt

Bread
2 medium-size potatoes
    (1 cup mashed)
2 packages (2 tablespoons)
    dry yeast
6 cups white flour, divided
    (approximately)
1½ tablespoons salt
4 to 5 tablespoons caraway seeds
cornmeal or vegetable cooking
    spray

¼ cup cold water
1 tablespoon cornstarch
1 cup boiling water

Begin making the rye sour 48 hours in advance. Combine ½ cup of the rye flour, yeast, 1 cup of the warm water, caraway seeds, and onion in a medium-size bowl and mix until smooth. The mixture should be soupy. Cover and let stand for 24 hours in a warm spot.

The next day, add 1¼ cups rye flour and ½ cup warm water. Stir until well blended and sprinkle the top with ¼ cup rye flour. Cover for 4 to 8 hours, or until the floured top appears cracked with fissures spread widely apart. Avoid letting the sour collapse. Add ¾ cup of the white flour and ½ cup warm water. Stir until well blended and sprinkle with ¼ cup rye flour. Let rise for 4 to 8 hours, or until fissures form. Add the remaining ¾ cup white flour and remaining ½ cup warm water. Stir and sprinkle with the remaining ¼ cup rye flour and let rise for another 4 to 8 hours.

To make the filling, combine all the ingredients in a small bowl and set aside.

To make the bread, cook the potatoes and drain, reserving 1 cup of the cooking water. Mash the potatoes. In a large bowl, dissolve the yeast in the warm potato water (105° to 120° F). When bubbles start to form, blend in the mashed potatoes and rye sour. Add 3 cups of the white flour, salt, and caraway seeds. Mix with a wooden spoon until the dough pulls away from the sides of the bowl, adding up to 3 more cups flour as needed. Turn the dough out onto a floured surface and knead for about 5 to 8 minutes. Knead in the filling and enough flour to make a soft, slightly sticky dough. Place the dough on an oiled surface, cover, and let rest for 15 minutes.

Preheat the oven to 200° F. Divide the dough into 3 parts. Either shape into round loaves and place on baking sheets sprinkled with corn-meal or place in loaf pans coated with vegetable cooking spray. Place in the oven, turn the temperature off, and leave the door open while the loaves rise for about 45 minutes. Remove from the oven, then preheat the oven to 375° F. Place an empty baking pan (about 10×8 inches) on the lower rack of the oven while it is heating.

Meanwhile, in a small bowl, combine the cold water and cornstarch. Add the boiling water and stir. With a pastry brush, coat the dough with the cornstarch mixture. Poke about 12 holes in each loaf with a skewer or peeled stick. Put about a dozen ice cubes in the baking pan and bake the loaves for 35 to 40 minutes, or until they sound hollow when tapped. Turn out onto wire racks, brush again with the cornstarch solution, and cool.

Paul C. Osterman, Poughkeepsie, New York
Dutchess County Fair, Rhinebeck, New York

Rye Bread

2 loaves

1 cup milk
2 teaspoons salt
3 tablespoons shortening
3 tablespoons plus 1 teaspoon
  molasses, divided
1 package (1 tablespoon) dry yeast

1 cup warm water (110° F)
2 cups medium rye flour
3 to 4½ cups white flour, divided
1 egg white beaten with
  1 tablespoon water

In the microwave oven, heat the milk, salt, shortening, and 3 tablespoons of the molasses for 1 minute. (You also may do this on the stovetop.) Pour into a large bowl and cool to lukewarm. Add the yeast and remaining 1 teaspoon molasses to the warm water. Stir and let proof for 10 minutes. Add the yeast mixture to the milk mixture and stir with a wire whisk. Add the rye flour and 2 cups of the white flour; stir with a wooden spoon. Continue adding white flour until the dough pulls away from the sides of the bowl. Turn the dough out onto a floured surface and knead for 10 minutes, adding white flour to prevent the dough from sticking to the surface. Place in a greased bowl, cover with plastic wrap, and let rise in a warm place until doubled in bulk, about 1 hour.

Punch the dough down and knead for about 30 seconds. Divide in half and let rest for 5 minutes. Form into 2 round loaves and place on a greased baking sheet. Cover with plastic wrap and let rise until doubled in bulk, about 30 minutes.

Preheat the oven to 350° F. Make 3 slashes in the top of each loaf and brush with the egg-water mixture. Bake for 35 to 45 minutes, or until the loaves sound hollow when tapped. Remove from the baking sheet and cool on wire racks.

David Oxley, Seattle, Washington
Western Washington Fair, Puyallup, Washington

Blue Ribbon Tip

BAKING WITH RYE FLOUR

Rye flour comes in many forms. Paul Osterman (see Sourdough Onion-Potato Rye Bread with Caraway, page 26) uses white rye flour to make his bread and believes it makes the best loaf. Our tester used dark rye, and it came out very well. Medium rye flour also will yield a tasty loaf. White rye and dark rye flours can be obtained from specialty baking shops or from health food stores.

Unlike wheat flour, rye flour contains no gluten, so it does not make a chewy bread. Making a good rye bread is always a careful balancing act, requiring enough rye flour to get a good rye flavor and enough wheat flour to give it an elastic texture. Extra care in proofing, kneading, and rising conditions will help to compensate for some of the elasticity lost by using rye flour. Give the bread extra time to rise if it needs it, and help the wheat flour do its job by kneading the dough especially well.

Dinner Rolls

4 dozen rolls

Long-time baker Elaine Janas guarantees that these perfect little rolls will disappear fast.

1 cup water
⅓ cup honey
¼ cup (½ stick) butter or
   margarine
4½ to 5 cups bread flour, divided
1½ teaspoons salt

2 packages (2 tablespoons) dry
   yeast
3 eggs
3 tablespoons butter, softened
melted butter

Heat the water, honey, and ¼ cup butter to 120° to 130° F. In a large bowl, blend 2 cups of the flour, salt, and yeast. Add the liquid and beat with an electric mixer on medium speed for 3 minutes. Beat in the eggs. Stir in enough of the remaining flour to make a soft dough. Turn out onto a floured surface and knead until smooth and elastic. Place in a greased bowl, cover, and let rise until doubled in bulk, about 1 hour.

Punch the dough down. Divide into 3 parts. Cover and let rest for 15 minutes. Roll each portion out into a 12-inch circle. Spread each round with 1 tablespoon of the softened butter. Cut each round into 16 wedges. Starting at the wide end, roll each wedge up. Place point side down on a greased baking sheet. Cover and let rise until doubled in bulk, about 30 minutes.

Preheat the oven to 375° F. Bake for 10 to 12 minutes. Immediately brush the tops of the rolls with melted butter.

Elaine Janas, Columbia Heights, Minnesota
Minnesota State Fair, St. Paul, Minnesota

Honey Oatmeal Bread

2 loaves

5¾ to 6¼ cups flour, divided
2 packages (2 tablespoons) dry
   yeast
1¾ cups water
1 cup plus 6 tablespoons
   quick-cooking oats, divided
½ cup honey

1 tablespoon salt
⅓ cup butter-flavored shortening
2 eggs
1 egg white beaten with
   1 tablespoon water
oats for sprinkling

Combine 2 cups of the flour with the yeast in a large mixer bowl. In a saucepan, combine the water, 1 cup of the oats, honey, salt, and shortening. Heat until the shortening is almost melted. Cool to 110° F and add to the flour mixture. Add the eggs and beat on low for 30 seconds and then on high for 3 minutes. Using a wooden spoon, stir in as much flour as possible. Turn out onto a lightly floured surface and knead in enough of the remaining flour to make a moderately stiff dough that is smooth and elastic. Shape into a ball and place in a greased bowl, turning once to grease the top. Cover and let rise in a warm place until doubled in bulk, about 90 minutes.

Punch the dough down and turn out onto a lightly floured surface. Divide into 2 parts. Cover and let rest for 10 minutes. Grease two 9×5-inch pans. Sprinkle 3 tablespoons of the remaining oats into each pan. Shape the dough into loaves and place in the pans. Cover and let rise until doubled in bulk, about 45 minutes.

Preheat the oven to 375° F. Brush the tops of the dough with the egg-water mixture. Sprinkle lightly with oats. Bake for 40 to 45 minutes. Cover loosely with aluminum foil during the last 15 minutes of baking to prevent overbrowning. Remove from the pans and cool on wire racks.

Sue Thomas, Indianapolis, Indiana
Indiana State Fair, Indianapolis, Indiana

Orange Bread

2 loaves

This tasty sweet bread goes perfectly with tea or coffee.

1¼ cups water	2 packages (2 tablespoons)
½ cup powdered milk	dry yeast
½ cup sugar	2 eggs
½ cup (1 stick) butter	1½ cups golden raisins
grated rind of 1 orange	1 cup confectioners' sugar
½ teaspoon ground ginger	½ cup walnuts, finely chopped
2 teaspoons salt	4 to 6 tablespoons orange juice
5 cups flour, divided	

Place the water, milk, sugar, butter, orange rind, ginger, and salt in a saucepan and heat to 110° to 120° F. Place 2½ cups of the flour and the yeast in a large bowl. Pour the warm liquid over the flour and yeast and mix well. Add the eggs and raisins. Add the remaining 2½ cups flour and mix well. Turn out onto a lightly floured surface and knead until soft and elastic. Place in a greased bowl, cover, and let rise until doubled in bulk, about 1 hour.

Knead the dough and divide into 2 parts. Shape each into a loaf and place in a greased 8½x4½-inch pan. Cover and let rise until doubled in bulk, about 30 minutes.

Preheat the oven to 350° F. Make 3 shallow slits in the top of each loaf. Bake for 30 minutes, or until golden brown. Remove from the pans and cool on wire racks.

Meanwhile, mix together the confectioners' sugar, walnuts, and enough orange juice to make a fairly thick glaze. Spoon gently over the warm loaves.

Kathleen Shangraw, Huntington, Vermont
Champlain Valley Fair and Exposition, Essex Junction, Vermont

Chapter 2

Quick Breads & Muffins

"Nearly eleven o'clock," said Pooh happily. "You're just in time for a little smackerel of something."

—A. A. MILNE (1882–1956)

Cranberry-Orange Scones

8 scones

This is the kind of recipe you'll make again and again because it is so easy and so good. Dried cranberries can be found in many supermarkets under the name "Craisins" and in most health food stores. You may use them in place of raisins in many recipes. Try them in oatmeal, too.

2 cups flour
1 tablespoon baking powder
½ teaspoon baking soda
¼ teaspoon salt
3 tablespoons sugar, divided
1 tablespoon grated orange rind

½ cup (1 stick) cold butter,
  cut up
⅔ cup buttermilk
1 cup dried cranberries
1 tablespoon milk

Preheat the oven to 425° F. Combine the flour, baking powder, baking soda, salt, 2 tablespoons of the sugar, and orange rind in a bowl or food processor. Cut in the butter with a pastry blender or food processor. Stir in the buttermilk and dried cranberries, mixing just until moistened. Turn the dough out onto a lightly floured surface. Knead 5 or 6 times. Pat into an 8-inch circle. Cut into 8 wedges and place 1 inch apart on a lightly greased baking sheet. Brush with the milk and sprinkle with the remaining 1 tablespoon sugar. Bake for 15 minutes, or until golden brown. Remove from the pan and cool on wire racks.

Diana Ferris, Red Hook, New York
Dutchess County Fair, Rhinebeck, New York

Cranberry-Ginger Bread

1 loaf

The lime juice and ginger make this batter smell delicious, and the end result is a very good, very different cranberry loaf. Our recipe tester says that next time she tries this recipe, she might use a little more lime juice and ginger and reduce the water proportionately.

2 cups flour	1 teaspoon grated lime rind
¾ cup sugar	1½ teaspoons grated
1½ teaspoons baking powder	fresh ginger
¾ teaspoon salt	1 tablespoon lime juice
½ teaspoon baking soda	¾ cup water
¼ cup (½ stick) butter or	1 cup fresh cranberries, chopped
margarine	½ cup nuts, chopped

Preheat the oven to 350° F. Place the flour, sugar, baking powder, salt, and baking soda in a mixing bowl or food processor. Cut in the butter until crumbly. Stir in the lime rind, ginger, lime juice, and water just to moisten. Stir in the cranberries and nuts and pour into a greased 9×5-inch pan. Bake for 55 to 65 minutes, or until golden brown and a toothpick inserted in the center comes out clean. Cool in the pan on a wire rack for 5 minutes. Remove from the pan and cool completely on the rack. Wrap in plastic wrap and let sit overnight.

Victoria Steponaitis, Middlebury, Connecticut
Cranberry Harvest Festival, Carver, Massachusetts

Irish Bread

2 loaves

The caraway seeds and sugar in this bread are a surprisingly delightful combination. Melissa Bouchard began baking bread at the age of 7, and at age 13 she entered in competition five ethnic recipes she'd never made before. This one received a blue ribbon. Delicious with a bowl of soup for supper.

1 cup raisins	1 cup sugar
1 cup milk	2 eggs
3½ to 4 cups flour, divided	1 teaspoon salt
½ cup (1 stick) butter or shortening	2 tablespoons baking powder
	1 to 3 tablespoons caraway seeds

Preheat the oven to 350° F. Soak the raisins in the milk for a few minutes. Drain, reserving the milk, and dredge the raisins with ½ cup of the flour. Beat the butter, sugar, eggs, and reserved milk. Combine 3 cups of the flour with the salt, baking powder, and caraway seeds. Add the flour mixture to the butter mixture and mix well. Add enough of the remaining flour to make a stiff dough. Stir in the raisins. Pour the batter into 2 greased 8½x4½-inch pans. Bake for 45 minutes, or until a toothpick inserted in the center comes out clean. Remove the bread from the pans and cool on wire racks. Wrap in a kitchen towel to prevent the crust from hardening.

Melissa Bouchard, Coventry, Rhode Island
Washington County Fair, Carolina, Rhode Island

Cheddar Cheese–Pepper Bread

1 loaf

½ cup (1 stick) butter
2½ cups flour
2½ teaspoons baking powder
1 to 1½ teaspoons freshly ground
 black pepper
¾ teaspoon baking soda

¾ teaspoon salt
2 cups shredded sharp Cheddar
 cheese (about 8 ounces)
2 eggs
1 cup (8 ounces) plain yogurt

Preheat the oven to 375° F. Butter and flour a 9×5-inch pan. Melt the butter in a small saucepan over low heat; set aside to cool. Combine the flour, baking powder, black pepper, baking soda, and salt in a large bowl. Stir in the cheese. In a medium-size bowl, lightly beat the eggs. Stir in the yogurt and melted butter. Add to the flour mixture, stirring just until moistened. Spoon into the prepared pan. Bake for 35 minutes, or until golden brown and a toothpick inserted in the center comes out clean. Cool in the pan on a wire rack for 10 minutes, then remove from the pan. Serve warm or toasted.

Georgeann Frajkar, North Arlington, New Jersey
Flemington Agricultural Fair, Flemington, New Jersey

Blue Ribbon Tip

PEPPER POWER

Pepper has had the greatest impact on world history of any spice. It was the search for pepper that motivated Christopher Columbus and other explorers to find new routes around the world, and pepper continues to far outsell all other spices. Peppercorns are the berries of the pepper plant and often are picked as soon as they appear on the vine. Look for tellicherry pepper, which is allowed to vine ripen, and therefore grows larger and more tangy than other pepper.

Date Bran Muffins

1 dozen muffins

1¼ cups flour
3 teaspoons baking powder
½ teaspoon salt
½ cup sugar
3 cups 100% bran cereal
  (not flakes)

1¼ cups milk
1 egg
⅓ cup vegetable oil
1 cup dates, chopped

Preheat the oven to 400° F. Grease 12 muffin cups. Stir together the flour, baking powder, salt, and sugar; set aside. Combine the cereal and milk and let stand for 1 to 2 minutes. Add the egg and oil; beat well. Stir in the dates. Add the dry ingredients and stir to combine. Pour into the muffin cups and bake for 20 to 25 minutes, or until golden brown. Remove from the pan immediately. Serve warm or at room temperature.

Dorothy Dillon, Indio, California
National Date Festival, Indio, California

Blue Ribbon Tip

BAKING SODA & BAKING POWDER

Baking soda is pure bicarbonate of soda, which, when combined with an acid such as lemon juice, buttermilk, or sugars, releases bubbles of carbon dioxide and makes a batter rise. Baking powder simply combines the acid and baking soda in one convenient package. Some double-acting baking powders contain sodium aluminum sulfate (SAS), which can react with an aluminum pan during baking, leaving a bitter aftertaste. This is not a problem with a phosphate-based baking powder such as Rumford, which does not contain SAS. Whereas baking soda has an unlimited shelf life as long as it stays dry, the acid ingredient(s) in baking powder can lose its strength in about a year.

Michigan Cherry Muffins

1 dozen muffins

These muffins have a great flavor and texture, and they are low in cholesterol, too!

vegetable cooking spray
1 cup flour
¾ cup oat bran
⅔ cup sugar
1 tablespoon baking powder
½ teaspoon salt
¾ cup skim milk
½ cup nonfat plain yogurt

⅓ cup margarine, melted and cooled
2 egg whites, slightly beaten
1 teaspoon almond extract
¾ cup dried cherries, chopped
⅓ cup pecans, chopped
2 teaspoons grated lemon rind

Preheat the oven to 400° F. Spray 12 muffin cups with vegetable cooking spray. In a medium-size bowl, combine the flour, oat bran, sugar, baking powder, and salt; mix well. In another bowl, combine the milk, yogurt, margarine, egg whites, and almond extract. Add to the flour mixture, stirring just until moistened. Fold in the cherries, pecans, and lemon rind. Fill the muffin cups two-thirds full. Bake for 20 to 25 minutes, or until golden brown. Remove immediately from the pan. Serve warm or at room temperature.

Robin Giordano, Traverse City, Michigan
National Cherry Festival, Traverse City, Michigan

Zucchini Bread

2 loaves

3 eggs
2 cups sugar
1 cup oil
1 tablespoon vanilla
2 cups grated zucchini
3 cups flour

1 teaspoon baking soda
1 teaspoon salt
1 tablespoon ground cinnamon
¼ teaspoon baking powder
½ cup nuts, chopped
cinnamon sugar

Preheat the oven to 350° F. Grease two 8½x4½-inch pans. Beat the eggs, sugar, oil, vanilla, and zucchini. Sift together the flour, baking soda, salt, cinnamon, and baking powder. Beat into the zucchini mixture. Stir in the nuts. Pour into the prepared pans and bake for 45 minutes, or until a toothpick inserted in the center comes out clean. Remove from the pans and cool on wire racks. Sprinkle cinnamon sugar over the tops of the warm loaves.

Sharon Nichols, Wellington, Kansas
Kansas Wheat Festival, Wellington, Kansas

Orange Nut Bread
with Orange Cream Cheese Spread

3 small loaves

These teatime treats are a favorite of guests at the Governor's Inn in Ludlow, Vermont. Innkeeper Deedy Marble serves them on antique plates garnished with orange nasturtiums and sprigs of fresh mint.

2 cups sifted flour	½ teaspoon vanilla
½ teaspoon salt	½ teaspoon orange extract
1 teaspoon baking powder	1 cup walnuts, chopped
¼ teaspoon baking soda	3 packages (8 ounces each)
⅔ cup granulated sugar	cream cheese
⅓ cup unsalted butter, softened	1 thin-skinned navel orange,
2 eggs	cut into chunks
1 cup freshly squeezed orange	3 to 4 tablespoons confectioners'
juice, with pulp	sugar

Preheat the oven to 350° F. Sift together the flour, salt, baking powder, and baking soda. Cream the granulated sugar and butter, then beat in the eggs one at a time. Add the orange juice alternately with the flour mixture. Add the vanilla, orange extract, and walnuts; stir well. Pour into 3 well-greased 6×3½-inch pans. Bake for about 40 minutes, or until a toothpick inserted in the center comes out clean. Remove from the pans and cool on wire racks. Wrap in plastic wrap and chill well before slicing.

Meanwhile, using a food processor equipped with a steel blade, combine the cream cheese, orange chunks, and confectioners' sugar. Refrigerate for a few hours to blend the flavors. Slice the bread thinly and make little sandwiches using the orange spread.

Deedy Marble, Ludlow, Vermont
Great New England Food Festival, Boston, Massachusetts

Banana Nut Bread

1 loaf

It's hard to beat this bread for rich banana flavor.

2 cups flour
1 teaspoon baking soda
⅛ teaspoon salt
½ cup vegetable oil
1 cup sugar

3 eggs, beaten
3 medium-size ripe bananas,
   mashed
2 tablespoons buttermilk
1 cup nuts, chopped

Preheat the oven to 350° F. Sift together the flour, baking soda, and salt. In another bowl, cream the oil and sugar. Add the eggs, bananas, and buttermilk; beat well. Stir into the dry ingredients, then stir in the nuts. Pour into a greased 9×5-inch pan. Bake for 1 hour, or until a toothpick inserted in the center comes out clean. Cool for 10 minutes in the pan, then remove from the pan and cool completely on a wire rack.

Tammy Reiss, Moore, Oklahoma
Oklahoma State Fair, Oklahoma City, Oklahoma

Chapter 3

Coffeecakes

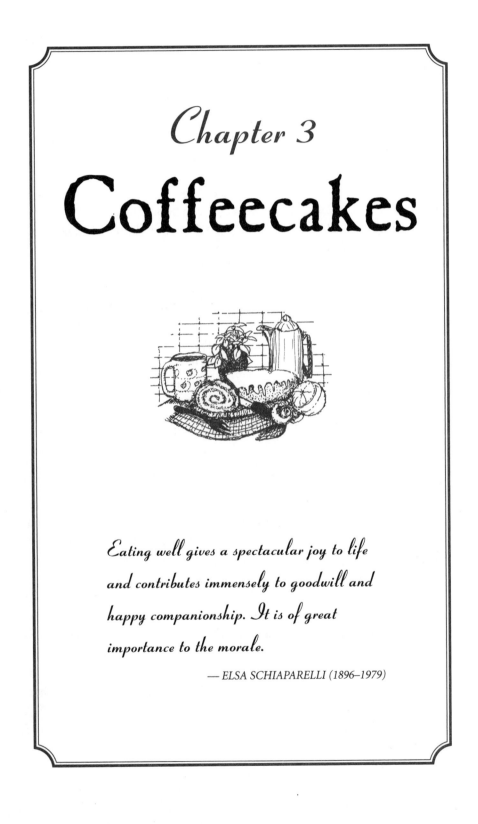

*Eating well gives a spectacular joy to life
and contributes immensely to goodwill and
happy companionship. It is of great
importance to the morale.*

— ELSA SCHIAPARELLI (1896–1979)

Danish Nut Loaf

4 loaves

Light and yummy, and not anywhere near as much work as these long instructions imply. Definitely a winner! (For tips on grinding nuts, see page 65.)

Dough
1 pound (4 sticks) butter, softened
4¾ cups flour, divided
2 packages (2 tablespoons)
   dry yeast
⅓ cup plus 1 teaspoon sugar,
   divided
½ cup warm water
   (105° to 115° F)
1 teaspoon salt
¾ cup milk (not skim)
2 eggs, slightly beaten

Filling
¼ cup honey
2 tablespoons butter or margarine
¼ cup milk
½ teaspoon vanilla
½ cup packed brown sugar
1 pound walnuts, ground

1 egg white, slightly beaten
¼ cup sugar
¼ cup ground walnuts

To make the dough, beat the butter and ½ cup of the flour together in a large bowl. (The electric mixer is helpful here.) Place the mixture between two sheets of wax paper. Roll out to a 12×10-inch rectangle. Place on a cookie sheet and refrigerate.

Sprinkle the yeast and 1 teaspoon of the sugar on the warm water. Stir and set aside until bubbly, about 10 minutes. In a large mixer bowl, combine the yeast mixture with 3 cups flour, the remaining ⅓ cup sugar, salt, milk, and eggs. Beat on medium for 3 minutes. Beat in the remaining 1¼ cups flour with a wooden spoon or with the dough hook of the electric mixer until the dough is shiny and elastic. (The dough will be soft.) Scrape down the sides of the bowl, cover with plastic wrap, and refrigerate for 30 minutes.

Turn the dough out onto a floured surface. Using flour as necessary to prevent sticking, roll out to a 22×14-inch rectangle. Peel the top sheet of wax paper off the butter mixture and place, butter side down, in the middle of the dough. Peel off the second sheet of paper and fold the uncovered dough over the butter to enclose it completely. Fold the dough in half, then in half again, making four layers. Sprinkle flour on any butter that may ooze out of the dough. Roll out to a 22×14-inch rectangle, using flour as necessary to prevent the dough from sticking. Repeat the folding and rolling 2 more times. If necessary, chill the dough between rollings. Place the dough in a large bowl. Cover tightly with plastic wrap and refrigerate overnight.

To make the filling, heat the honey, butter, and milk just until warm. Add the vanilla. Blend in the brown sugar and walnuts. (Do not do this a day ahead, or the consistency will not be right.)

Cut the dough into quarters. Roll one piece of dough out to a 12-inch square. (Making this piece really square will ensure a beautiful, even-looking loaf.) Keep the other pieces refrigerated. Cut the square into three 12x4-inch strips. Spread a scant ⅓ cup filling down the center of each strip. Roll up lengthwise, jellyroll style. Place the 3 strips side by side and braid together. Tuck the loose ends underneath and gently place in a greased 8½x4½-inch pan. Repeat with the remaining dough. Let rise until doubled in bulk, about 45 minutes to 1 hour. (The dough will not reach the top of the pan.)

Preheat the oven to 375° F. Brush the dough with the beaten egg white. Combine the sugar and walnuts and sprinkle over the dough. Bake for 35 to 45 minutes, or until golden brown. Cool in the pans, then gently turn out onto wire racks.

Fran Hurayt, Austintown, Ohio
Canfield Fair, Canfield, Ohio

Blue Ribbon Tip

SAVE SOME FOR LATER

Many of us do not need four of these loaves at once. It is very easy to wrap and freeze half of this dough to be used for another occasion. In this case, make just half of the filling and topping. The night before you want to assemble the loaves, transfer the dough from the freezer to the refrigerator.

Apple-Walnut Poppy Seed Coffeecake

10 to 12 servings

Our recipe tester says, "This was quite good — a little better, I think, than the average sour cream coffeecake. The apples make it nice and moist, and it didn't last very long around my house."

½ cup vegetable oil
1 cup granulated sugar
2 eggs
1 teaspoon vanilla
2 cups flour
1 teaspoon baking powder
1 teaspoon baking soda
¼ teaspoon salt
3 tablespoons poppy seeds

1 cup sour cream
2 cups peeled, cored, and finely chopped apples
1 cup nuts, chopped
¾ cup lightly packed brown sugar
1 teaspoon ground cinnamon
¼ cup (½ stick) butter, melted

Preheat the oven to 350° F. Grease and flour a 13×9-inch baking pan. Mix together the oil and granulated sugar. Beat in the eggs and vanilla; set aside. Sift together the flour, baking powder, baking soda, and salt. Stir in the poppy seeds. Add to the oil mixture alternately with the sour cream, beginning and ending with the flour mixture. Fold in the apples and pour into the prepared pan. Combine the nuts, brown sugar, cinnamon, and butter. Sprinkle over the batter. Bake for 35 to 45 minutes, or until a toothpick inserted in the center comes out clean. Cool in the pan for 10 minutes, then serve.

Julie DeMatteo, Clementon, New Jersey
The Old Farmer's Almanac Recipe Contest, Dublin, New Hampshire

Sour Cream Coffeecake

12 servings

Batter
½ cup (1 stick) butter
1 cup sugar
1 teaspoon vanilla
2 eggs
2 cups flour
1 teaspoon baking soda
1 teaspoon baking powder
½ teaspoon salt

1 teaspoon ground cinnamon
1 cup sour cream

Topping
½ cup chopped pecans
1½ teaspoons ground cinnamon
½ teaspoon vanilla
⅓ cup sugar

10 to 12 pecan halves

Preheat the oven to 350° F. Grease an angel food cake pan.

To make the batter, cream the butter and sugar. Add the vanilla and eggs and beat. Sift together the flour, baking soda, baking powder, salt, and cinnamon. Add to the butter mixture and mix well. Add the sour cream.

To make the topping, mix together all the ingredients.

Place the pecan halves neatly on the bottom of the prepared pan. Pour half of the batter into the pan and sprinkle half of the topping over it. Pour in the remaining batter and sprinkle with the remaining topping. Bake for 40 to 45 minutes, or until a toothpick inserted in the cake comes out clean.

Mary Schmaltz, Pueblo, Colorado
Colorado State Fair, Pueblo, Colorado

Orange Bowknot Rolls

20 rolls

Marjorie Johnson has loved baking since she was eight. She was one of six daughters and her mother's "best helper" when it came to the baking chores. Marjorie has won 1,725 ribbons in various competitions. Her goal is to win 2,000 ribbons by the year 2000. These delicious rolls are light and not too sweet — great for weekend company.

Rolls
1¼ cups warm water
2 packages (2 tablespoons)
    dry yeast
⅓ cup nonfat powdered milk
½ cup shortening
⅓ cup sugar
1 teaspoon salt

2 eggs, beaten
¼ cup orange juice
2 tablespoons grated orange rind
5 to 6 cups flour, divided

Icing
2 tablespoons orange juice
1 teaspoon grated orange rind
1 cup confectioners' sugar

To make the rolls, pour the water into a large mixer bowl and sprinkle with the yeast. Add the milk, shortening, sugar, salt, eggs, orange juice, orange rind, and 3 cups of the flour. Blend on low, then beat on medium for 3 minutes. Add enough of the remaining flour to make a soft dough, either using the mixer's bread hook or stirring it in by hand. Turn the dough out onto a lightly floured surface and knead until smooth and elastic. Place in a greased bowl. Cover and let rise in a warm place until doubled in bulk, about 1½ hours.

Punch the dough down. Roll out to a ½-inch-thick rectangle that measures about 20x10 inches. Cut crosswise into ½-inch strips. Tie each strip into a knot and arrange on greased baking sheets. Cover and let rise until doubled in bulk, about 30 to 40 minutes.

Preheat the oven to 400° F. Bake for 8 to 10 minutes, or until golden brown. Cool on wire racks.

To make the icing, combine all the ingredients until well blended. Brush over the tops of the rolls.

Marjorie Johnson, Robbinsdale, Minnesota
Minnesota State Fair, St. Paul, Minnesota

Coffeecake Muffins

1 dozen muffins

These tasty muffins live up to their name. You'll find they are a winner with kids because of their sweet flavor.

Batter
1½ cups flour
½ cup sugar
2 teaspoons baking powder
½ teaspoon salt
½ cup vegetable oil
1 egg, slightly beaten
⅓ cup milk
1 teaspoon almond extract

Topping
¼ cup firmly packed brown sugar
¼ cup walnuts, chopped
¼ cup dried cherries, chopped
3 tablespoons flour
1 tablespoon butter or margarine, melted

Icing
½ cup confectioners' sugar
1 tablespoon milk
1 teaspoon almond extract

Preheat the oven to 350° F. Grease 12 muffin cups.

To make the batter, combine the flour, sugar, baking powder, and salt in a large bowl; mix well. In another bowl, combine the oil, egg, milk, and almond extract. Add to the flour mixture, stirring just until moistened.

To make the topping, combine the brown sugar, walnuts, cherries, and flour in a small bowl. Stir in the melted butter. Mix until crumbly.

Distribute half of the batter among the muffin cups. Sprinkle with half of the topping. Add the remaining batter and topping. Bake for 15 to 20 minutes, or until a toothpick inserted in the center comes out clean. Remove from the pan and cool on wire racks.

To make the icing, combine all the ingredients, mixing until smooth. Drizzle over the warm muffins. Serve warm or at room temperature.

Anne Smith, Traverse City, Michigan
National Cherry Festival, Traverse City, Michigan

Apricot Tea Ring

2 coffeecakes

Dough
½ cup milk
½ cup water
⅓ cup butter or margarine
4 cups flour, divided
⅓ cup sugar
1 teaspoon salt
2 packages (2 tablespoons)
   dry yeast
2 eggs
1 teaspoon grated orange rind
⅛ teaspoon ground mace

Filling
1¼ cups dried apricots, chopped
¼ cup water

¼ cup sugar
¼ teaspoon ground cinnamon
⅛ teaspoon salt
1 teaspoon grated lemon rind
1 tablespoon lemon juice

Glaze
1 cup confectioners' sugar
1 tablespoon milk or water
½ teaspoon butter, melted and
   cooled
½ teaspoon vanilla

toasted sliced almonds

To make the dough, heat the milk, water, and butter to 120° to 130° F. In a large bowl, combine 2 cups of the flour, sugar, salt, and yeast. Add the hot liquid and beat for 3 minutes. Add the eggs, orange rind, and mace; beat well. Stir in the remaining 2 cups flour to make a soft dough. Turn out onto a lightly floured surface and knead until smooth, 3 to 5 minutes. Place in a greased bowl, cover, and let rise until doubled in bulk, about 1 hour.

Meanwhile, make the filling. Combine all the ingredients in a saucepan. Cook over medium heat, stirring constantly, until thickened, about 10 minutes. Cool.

Punch the dough down. Divide into 2 parts. Cover and let rest for 15 minutes. Roll each part out into a 22×7-inch rectangle. Spread each rectangle with about ⅔ cup filling. Starting with the long side, roll up jellyroll style. Place in a ring shape on a greased baking sheet. At ½-inch intervals, make slashes down through the dough to within 1 inch of the pan. Cover and let rise until doubled in bulk, about 45 minutes.

Preheat the oven to 375° F. Bake for 25 to 30 minutes, or until golden brown.

Meanwhile, make the glaze. Combine all the ingredients until creamy and spread on the coffeecake while it is still slightly warm. Sprinkle with the almonds.

Elaine Janas, Columbia Heights, Minnesota
Minnesota State Fair, St. Paul, Minnesota

Blue Ribbon Tip

FREEZING BAKED COFFEECAKES

If you don't want to serve both these coffeecakes on the same day, it is easy to freeze one for later use. Wrap the unglazed coffeecake in aluminum foil and put it in a plastic bag, then freeze it. To thaw the coffeecake, remove it from the freezer and let sit on the counter the night before you wish to serve it. Place it in a 200° F oven for 30 minutes, still wrapped in aluminum foil. Glaze and serve.

Bavarian Coffeecake

8 to 10 servings

This coffeecake looks wonderful and tastes just the same. For fruit lovers, the filling can accommodate another apple.

Dough
1 cup (2 sticks) butter, softened
¾ cup sugar
2 tablespoons sour cream
2 eggs, beaten
1 teaspoon vanilla
2¾ cups flour
2 teaspoons baking powder

Filling
2½ cups peeled, cored, and sliced
   baking apples
1 teaspoon ground cinnamon
½ cup golden raisins

2 tablespoons sugar

Preheat the oven to 350° F.

To make the dough, cream the butter and sugar. Mix in the sour cream, eggs, and vanilla. Add the flour and baking powder. (The dough will be soft and pliable.) Divide in half. Pat out one half to fit the bottom and sides of a greased 10-inch springform pan. Form an edge all around and puncture the bottom with a fork in a few places.

To make the filling, place the apples in concentric circles on the dough. Sprinkle with the cinnamon and raisins.

Pat out the remaining dough and cut into 1-inch-wide strips. Weave into a lattice over the apples. Sprinkle with the sugar and bake for about 1 hour, or until the apples are tender and the cake is golden brown. Serve warm.

Karin Gaysek, Kitchener, Ontario
The Old Farmer's Almanac Recipe Contest, Dublin, New Hampshire

Chapter 4

Frosted Cakes

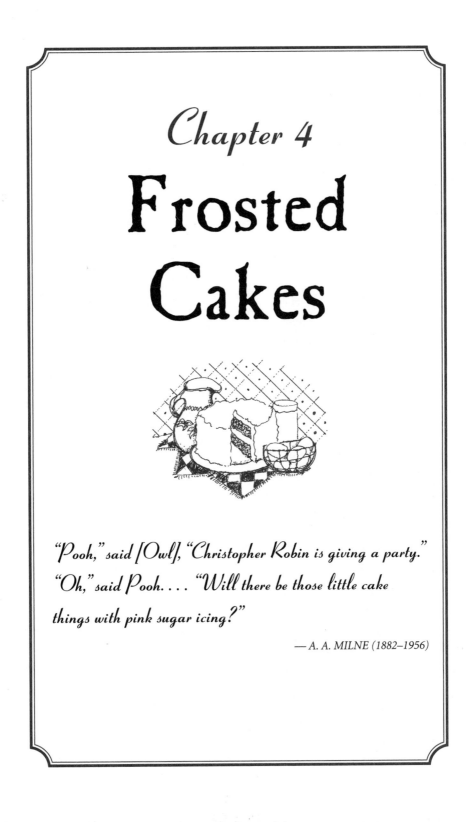

"Pooh," said [Owl], "Christopher Robin is giving a party."
"Oh," said Pooh. . . . "Will there be those little cake
things with pink sugar icing?"

— A. A. MILNE (1882–1956)

Hungarian Nut Torte

8 to 10 servings

This heirloom recipe combines an Old World torte with an American-style frosting. For a more traditional presentation, try substituting a chocolate glaze such as the one for Swiss Chocolate Cake on page 64.

Torte
6 eggs, separated
$\frac{7}{8}$ cup sugar
2 tablespoons rum
$\frac{1}{2}$ cup fine unsalted cracker crumbs (about 12 crackers)
$\frac{1}{4}$ cup grated unsweetened chocolate (about 1 ounce)
$\frac{3}{4}$ cup walnuts, chopped
$\frac{1}{2}$ teaspoon baking powder
$\frac{1}{4}$ teaspoon salt

$\frac{1}{2}$ teaspoon ground cinnamon
$\frac{1}{4}$ teaspoon ground cloves
$\frac{1}{4}$ teaspoon ground nutmeg

Frosting
$\frac{1}{3}$ cup butter, softened
3 cups confectioners' sugar, sifted
1 teaspoon vanilla
2 to 3 tablespoons milk or cream

$\frac{1}{2}$ cup walnuts, chopped
$\frac{1}{2}$ cup whipping cream, whipped

To make the torte, preheat the oven to 325° F. Beat the egg yolks until light. Add the sugar gradually and beat until well blended. Stir in the rum. In another bowl, combine the crumbs, chocolate, walnuts, baking powder, salt, cinnamon, cloves, and nutmeg. Add to the egg mixture and blend thoroughly. With clean beaters, beat the egg whites until stiff and fold into the batter. Pour into an ungreased 9-inch springform pan and bake for 35 to 45 minutes, or until a toothpick inserted in the center comes out clean. Cool in the pan on a wire rack for about 45 minutes. Remove the sides of the pan.

To make the frosting, beat the butter, confectioners' sugar, vanilla, and enough milk or cream to achieve a spreading consistency. Spread on the sides of the torte.

Pat the walnuts on the frosting. Pipe the whipped cream around the top edge.

Helen L. Harter, Rome, New York
The Old Farmer's Almanac Recipe Contest, Dublin, New Hampshire

Cream Cheese Cake

10 to 12 servings

A moist cake with a richer flavor than the average white cake.

Cake
1/2 cup (1 stick) butter, softened
1 package (8 ounces) cream
    cheese, softened
1 1/4 cups sugar
2 eggs
1 teaspoon vanilla
1/2 cup milk
2 cups flour
2 teaspoons baking powder
1/2 teaspoon baking soda
1/2 teaspoon salt

Filling
2 packages (8 ounces each) cream
    cheese, softened
1/2 cup fruit preserves

Frosting
2 packages (8 ounces each) cream
    cheese, softened
1 cup confectioners' sugar
1 teaspoon vanilla

To make the cake, preheat the oven to 350° F. Grease and flour 2 nine-inch round cake pans. Cream the butter and cream cheese until fluffy and light. Add all the remaining ingredients. Mix on low for 30 seconds. Beat on medium for 3 minutes, scraping the bowl occasionally. Pour into the prepared pans and bake for 30 to 35 minutes, or until a toothpick inserted in the center comes out clean. Cool in the pans on wire racks for 5 minutes. Remove from the pans and cool completely on racks.

To make the filling, blend the cream cheese and preserves until smooth. Spread thickly on top of one layer and place the other layer on it.

To make the frosting, blend all the ingredients until smooth. Frost the sides and top of the cake. Keep refrigerated until serving time.

Robin Laabs, Milwaukee, Wisconsin
Wisconsin State Fair, West Allis, Wisconsin

Blue Ribbon Tip

ALL FLOUR IS NOT CREATED EQUAL

All-purpose flour sounds like the sort of thing that ought to be pretty much the same anywhere. However, this turns out not to be true. All-purpose flour can be made from either hard wheat or a mixture of hard and soft wheats. This difference can dramatically affect the level of gluten in the finished product. For example, all-purpose flour in the North tends to be made with more hard wheat, and all-purpose flour in the South and West tends to have more soft wheat in it.

Because "hardness" is a measure of protein content, not texture, all-purpose flour made from hard wheat has a higher protein content than flour made from a blend of wheats or flour made from soft wheat, such as cake flour (see page 62). Hard-wheat flours have less starch and form strong gluten, giving structure to yeast breads. However, in making cakes, this means that the more you beat the batter, the more you develop the gluten, which can result in a tougher texture. Denser cakes, such as pound cakes, and cakes with particulates such as poppy seeds or nuts, turn out well with all-purpose flour.

Moist Chocolate Cake with Cocoa Butter Frosting

10 to 12 servings

Cake
2 cups flour
1 teaspoon salt
1 teaspoon baking powder
2 teaspoons baking soda
¾ cup unsweetened cocoa
2 cups sugar
1 cup vegetable oil
1 cup hot coffee
1 cup milk

2 eggs
1 teaspoon vanilla

Frosting
⅓ cup butter, softened
⅓ cup unsweetened cocoa
2 cups confectioners' sugar
1½ teaspoons vanilla
2 tablespoons milk
   (approximately)

To make the cake, preheat the oven to 325° F. Grease and flour 2 nine-inch round cake pans. In a mixer bowl, sift together the flour, salt, baking powder, baking soda, cocoa, and sugar. Add the oil, coffee, and milk. Beat for 2 minutes. Add the eggs and vanilla and beat for 2 minutes more. (The batter will be thin.) Pour into the prepared pans and bake for 25 to 35 minutes, or until a toothpick inserted in the center comes out clean. Cool in the pans on wire racks for 10 minutes. Remove from the pans and cool completely on racks before frosting.

To make the frosting, use an electric mixer to cream the butter and cocoa. Beat in the confectioners' sugar. Beat in the vanilla and enough milk to make the frosting of spreading consistency. Frost the cake.

Carolyn Moreton, Flemington, New Jersey
Flemington Agricultural Fair, Flemington, New Jersey

Peanut Butter Chocolate Chip Cupcakes

1 dozen large or 2 dozen small cupcakes

These delicious cupcakes are a guaranteed kid pleaser. The cook makes them for her sons' classroom parties.

Cupcakes
½ cup creamy peanut butter
½ cup (1 stick) butter, softened
1½ cups brown sugar
2 eggs
1 teaspoon vanilla
2 cups flour
½ teaspoon salt
1½ teaspoons baking powder
¾ cup milk
½ cup semisweet chocolate chips

Frosting
⅓ cup butter, softened
⅓ cup unsweetened cocoa
2 cups confectioners' sugar
1½ teaspoons vanilla
2 tablespoons milk

To make the cupcakes, preheat the oven to 375° F. Line muffin cups with paper liners. Cream the peanut butter, butter, and brown sugar until fluffy. Beat in the eggs and vanilla. Sift together the flour, salt, and baking powder. Add to the batter alternately with the milk. Stir in the chocolate chips. Fill the muffin cups one-half to three-quarters full. Bake for 20 minutes, or until a toothpick inserted in the center comes out clean. Cool completely.

To make the frosting, cream the butter until fluffy. Beat in the cocoa. Beat in the confectioners' sugar. Add the vanilla and milk and beat to spreading consistency. Frost the cupcakes.

Kate Ashenden, Shelburne, Massachusetts
Shelburne Grange Fair, Shelburne, Massachusetts

Date and Walnut Cake

12 servings

Cake
1 cup dates, chopped
1 teaspoon baking soda
1 cup boiling water
1 tablespoon butter
1 cup sugar
1 egg
1⅓ cups flour
½ cup walnuts, chopped

Frosting
1 package (8 ounces) cream
  cheese, softened
1 box (1 pound) confectioners'
  sugar

candied cherries (optional)
walnut halves (optional)

To make the cake, preheat the oven to 350° F. Grease a 9-inch round cake pan or an 8½x4½-inch loaf pan. Place the dates and baking soda in a small bowl and pour the boiling water over them. Let stand for 10 minutes. Cream the butter and sugar. Add the date mixture and egg and beat well. Add the flour and chopped walnuts and pour into the prepared pan. Bake the round layer for 30 to 40 minutes or the loaf for 50 to 60 minutes, or until a toothpick inserted in the center comes out clean. Let cool in the pan for 10 minutes. Remove from the pan and cool on a wire rack.

To make the frosting, beat the cream cheese, adding the confectioners' sugar gradually. Beat to spreading consistency. Spread on the thoroughly cooled cake. Garnish with candied cherries and walnut halves if desired.

Nancy McDowell, Desert Center, California
National Date Festival, Indio, California

Chocolate Torte
with Vanilla Sauce and Raspberries

8 to 12 servings

This dense and superchocolaty torte should satisfy the most confirmed chocolate maniac.

Torte

9 squares (9 ounces) semisweet
  chocolate, coarsely chopped
3 tablespoons raspberry liqueur
2 tablespoons milk
14 tablespoons unsalted butter,
  cut into tablespoon-size pieces
1 cup sugar, divided
13 tablespoons flour, sifted
5 eggs, separated
pinch of salt
pinch of cream of tartar

Glaze

6 tablespoons whipping cream
2 tablespoons raspberry liqueur
8 squares (8 ounces) semisweet
  chocolate, coarsely chopped

Vanilla Sauce

2 cups heavy cream
2 teaspoons vanilla
2 eggs
½ cup sugar

2 cups fresh raspberries

To make the torte, preheat the oven to 350° F. Butter a 9-inch spring-form pan or round cake pan with 2-inch sides. Line the bottom with wax paper. Butter the paper and dust with flour. Melt the chocolate with the liqueur and milk in the top of a double boiler. Add the butter one piece at a time, whisking until melted. Remove from the heat and whisk in ¾ cup of the sugar, flour, and egg yolks. Beat the egg whites with the salt and cream of tartar until soft peaks form. Add the remaining ¼ cup sugar 1 table-spoon at a time and beat until stiff but not dry. Whisk the chocolate mixture lightly, then fold in one-fourth of the egg whites. Fold the chocolate mixture back into the remaining whites. Pour into the prepared pan. Bake for about 1¼ hours, or until the center feels firm. (The top will crack.) Cool in the pan on a wire rack for 15 minutes. Turn out onto the rack, remove the wax paper, and turn over onto another rack. Cool completely.

To make the glaze, scald the cream with the liqueur in a heavy sauce-pan. Remove from the heat. Add the chocolate a little at a time, stirring until melted and heating slightly if necessary. Cool until thick enough to spread.

To make the vanilla sauce, combine the cream and vanilla in a saucepan. Heat just until boiling. Remove from the heat. In a large bowl, beat the eggs and sugar together. Add the hot cream in a slow stream, whisking steadily. Return the mixture to the saucepan. Cook over moderate heat, stirring with a wooden spoon, until thickened. Pour into a stainless steel bowl and set in a larger bowl of ice water. When cold, cover and refrigerate.

Invert the cake, flat side up, onto a platter. Spread the glaze evenly over the sides and top. Refrigerate until the glaze is firm. Serve at room temperature with the vanilla sauce and fresh raspberries.

Marilyn Neumayer, Manchester, Connecticut
Great New England Food Festival,
Boston, Massachusetts

Blue Ribbon Tip

SERVING A PRETTY CAKE

To keep the bottom of a frosted or glazed cake neat, place four strips of wax paper around and just under the bottom of the cake before frosting or glazing. Wait for the frosting or glaze to set completely, slide a knife carefully around the bottom of the cake, and gently pull out the wax paper. The edge of the cake and the platter will be nice and neat.

Blue Ribbon Tip

CAKE FLOUR:
THE BAKER'S SECRET INGREDIENT

One thing immediately apparent about cake flour is that its texture is much finer than that of all-purpose flour. But there is more to it than simply being finely milled. Cake flour is always made from soft wheat. Compared to hard wheat, soft wheat contains a little less of the two proteins that, when combined with water, form gluten. This means that cake flour is less likely to form elastic sheets of gluten that will interfere with the fast leavening action of baking powder or soda. Cake flour also has been chlorinated to permit a better distribution of the bubbles formed by the baking powder and soda, yielding a moist, velvety texture. Professional bakers almost always use cake flour to get that distinctive light texture we associate with bakery cakes.

If you substitute all-purpose flour for cake flour, use 2 tablespoons less flour per cup. Or use 2 tablespoons less all-purpose flour per cup of cake flour and add 2 tablespoons of cornstarch, which will enhance the sweetness of the cake.

Ultimately, it's a matter of taste: Choose cake flour if you prefer a high volume and airy texture. Choose an unbleached, high-quality all-purpose flour for a hearty, moist cake that will still taste good.

Forest Chiffon Cake

12 servings

Cake

2¼ cups cake flour
¾ cup granulated sugar
¾ cup firmly packed brown sugar
3 teaspoons baking powder
1 teaspoon salt
¾ cup cold water
½ cup vegetable oil
2 teaspoons maple flavoring
2 teaspoons black walnut extract
5 egg yolks
1 cup egg whites (about 8 eggs)
½ teaspoon cream of tartar
1 cup walnuts, finely chopped

Frosting

1 cup (2 sticks) butter or
    margarine, softened
3 cups confectioners' sugar
3 tablespoons firmly packed
    brown sugar
2 tablespoons maple syrup
2 teaspoons black walnut extract
1 to 2 tablespoons milk (optional)

¼ cup walnuts, chopped
    (optional)

To make the cake, preheat the oven to 325° F. Combine the flour, granulated sugar, brown sugar, baking powder, and salt in a large bowl. Using a wooden spoon, beat in the water, oil, maple flavoring, black walnut extract, and egg yolks until smooth. In another large bowl, beat the egg whites and cream of tartar until stiff peaks form. Gradually pour the batter over the egg whites, folding them in with a rubber spatula until just blended. Fold in the walnuts. Pour into an ungreased 10-inch tube pan. Bake for 55 minutes. Increase the oven temperature to 350° F and bake for 10 to 15 minutes more, or until the top springs back when lightly touched. Immediately turn the cake upside down onto a glass bottle or metal funnel. Let hang for about 2 hours, or until the cake is completely cool. Remove from the pan.

To make the frosting, beat the butter for 30 seconds. Add the confectioners' sugar and beat on low until fluffy. Add the brown sugar, maple syrup, and black walnut extract. Beat on high until smooth, creamy, and thick enough to spread, adding enough milk (if necessary) to achieve a spreading consistency. Frost the cake. Sprinkle with walnuts if desired.

Lilly R. Koski, Pueblo, Colorado
Colorado State Fair, Pueblo, Colorado

Swiss Chocolate Cake

12 servings

This is a true, flourless torte. Your guests will feel as though they have dropped into a coffee shop in old Vienna when they taste this scrumptious, light confection.

Cake	Glaze
2 cups ground toasted hazelnuts	4 squares (4 ounces) semisweet
3 teaspoons baking powder	chocolate
4 squares (4 ounces) semisweet	¼ cup water
chocolate	2 tablespoons butter or margarine
½ cup (1 stick) butter or	¼ cup confectioners' sugar, sifted
margarine	
1 cup sugar	½ cup toasted hazelnuts, chopped
6 eggs, separated	(optional)
1 teaspoon vanilla	

To make the cake, preheat the oven to 375° F. Trace the bottom of an 8- or 9-inch springform pan on wax paper and cut out the circle. Grease the pan, place the wax paper in the pan, and grease the paper. Combine the hazelnuts and baking powder in a small bowl. Melt the chocolate in the top of a double boiler. Cool. Cream the butter and sugar until fluffy. Beat in the egg yolks one at a time. Add the vanilla and melted chocolate and beat well. Stir in the hazelnut mixture.

With clean beaters, beat the egg whites until stiff but not dry. Stir about one-third of the egg whites into the hazelnut mixture. Fold in the remaining egg whites as gently as possible. Pour the batter into the prepared pan. Bake for 1 hour, or until a toothpick inserted in the center comes out clean. (The cake will fall in the center.) Cool in the pan on a wire rack. Remove from the pan and discard the wax paper.

To make the glaze, melt the chocolate with the water in the top of a double boiler. Stir in the butter and confectioners' sugar until smooth and blended. Spread a thin layer on the sides of the thoroughly cooled cake. Spread the remaining glaze on top. Garnish the sides with chopped hazelnuts if desired.

Nicole Primeau, Springfield, Oregon
Springfield Filbert Festival, Springfield, Oregon

Blue Ribbon Tip

TOASTING & GRINDING NUTS

To toast hazelnuts, also called filberts, place the whole nuts in a baking pan. Bake in a 350° F oven for 10 to 15 minutes. Roll the hot nuts in a wet towel to remove as many of the husks as possible.

To get the right texture for ground nuts, it is necessary to use the kind of grater commonly used for Parmesan cheese. A food processor will pulverize the nuts into small enough pieces, but it also will release too much of the oil. Hand-chopping will not get the pieces small or even enough. One cup of toasted hazelnuts should yield 2 cups of ground nuts.

Nany's Caramel–Peanut Butter Cake

10 to 16 servings

Terri Spitler created this cake in honor of her grandmother Mildred Snell. It is an adaptation of a cake her grandmother made often. This one is a real show-stopper because it contains five layers! (If you don't have 5 eight-inch pans, plan to bake the layers in batches.)

Cake
1 cup shortening
2½ cups sugar
6 eggs
3 cups flour, sifted
1 teaspoon baking powder
½ teaspoon salt
1 cup buttermilk
1 teaspoon vanilla

Filling
1 package (8 ounces) cream
  cheese, softened
¼ cup (½ stick) butter or
  margarine
1 box (1 pound) confectioners'
  sugar

½ cup creamy peanut butter
½ teaspoon vanilla

Frosting
½ cup (1 stick) butter or
  margarine
1½ cups lightly packed brown
  sugar
¼ cup light corn syrup
1 box (1 pound) confectioners'
  sugar
⅓ cup evaporated milk
1 teaspoon vanilla
1 cup extra-crunchy peanut
  butter

To make the cake, preheat the oven to 400° F. Grease 5 eight-inch round cake pans. Cut 5 circles out of wax paper to line the pans. Grease the paper and flour the pans and paper. Beat the shortening until fluffy. Gradually add the sugar. When well mixed, add the eggs one at a time, mixing well after each addition. Sift together the flour, baking powder, and salt. Add to the egg mixture 1 cup at a time, alternating with the buttermilk. Add the vanilla and mix only until combined. Pour into the prepared pans, using a heaping ½ cup for each layer. Spread to the edges of the pans and smooth. Bake for about 20 minutes, or until a toothpick inserted in the center comes out clean. Remove from the pans to wire racks. Remove the wax paper and cool completely.

To make the filling, cream the cream cheese and butter until well blended. Add the confectioners' sugar and continue beating until creamy. Add the peanut butter and vanilla. Spread on one cake layer. Place another layer on top and spread with filling. Continue stacking and spreading filling between the layers.

To make the frosting, melt the butter with the brown sugar and corn syrup in a saucepan. Bring to a boil. Remove from the heat, add the confectioners' sugar, evaporated milk, vanilla, and peanut butter. Beat until creamy. Spread on the top and sides of the cake.

Terri Spitler, Dothan, Alabama
National Peanut Festival, Dothan, Alabama

Linzertorte Cake

12 to 16 servings

This cake makes a very dramatic and impressive finale for any special dinner, looking as though it came straight out of a fancy European bakery. Your friends will surely award it a blue ribbon. Well worth the effort.

Cake
1 cup toasted hazelnuts
2 cups flour
1 tablespoon baking powder
1½ teaspoons Chinese five-spice powder
½ teaspoon ground nutmeg
½ teaspoon salt
¾ cup (1½ sticks) unsalted butter, softened
1½ cups sugar
3 egg yolks
2 teaspoons vanilla
1 teaspoon almond extract
1¼ cups whole milk
5 egg whites, at room temperature

Frosting
6 ounces good quality white chocolate
3 packages (8 ounces each) cream cheese, softened
9 tablespoons unsalted butter, softened
1½ cups confectioners' sugar
2¼ teaspoons vanilla
½ teaspoon almond extract

1 cup raspberry preserves, stirred to soften, divided
1½ cups toasted hazelnuts, finely chopped

To make the cake, preheat the oven to 350° F. Butter a 15x10-inch jellyroll pan. Line the pan with parchment or wax paper and grease the paper. Flour the pan and paper. Finely grind the nuts with the flour in a blender. (Be sure not to overprocess. For more information on working with nuts, see page 65.) Transfer to a medium-size bowl. Mix in the baking powder, five-spice powder, nutmeg, and salt. Using an electric mixer, beat the butter and sugar until well blended. Beat in the egg yolks, vanilla, and almond extract. On low speed, beat in the dry ingredients alternately with the milk, beating just until combined. The batter will be thick.

Using a clean bowl and beaters, beat the egg whites until stiff peaks form. Fold one-third of the whites into the batter. Fold in the remaining whites carefully. Spread the batter in the prepared pan. Bake until a tooth pick inserted in the center comes out clean, about 25 minutes. Cool in the pan on a wire rack for 20 minutes. Remove from the pan onto a layer of wax paper or aluminum foil on a wire rack. Carefully peel off the parchment or wax paper on the bottom. Cool completely.

To make the frosting, melt the white chocolate in the top of a double boiler. Cool to barely lukewarm. Using an electric mixer, beat the cream cheese and butter in a large bowl. Beat in the white chocolate, then the confectioners' sugar, vanilla, and almond extract. Work quickly to prevent the chocolate from setting.

Using a serrated knife, carefully cut the cake crosswise into three 10×5-inch rectangles. Carefully place one rectangle on a platter. Spread ¾ cup frosting over the cake. Drizzle with ¼ cup of the raspberry preserves. Top with a second cake layer and spread with ¾ cup frosting and drizzle with ¼ cup preserves. Top with a third cake layer. Place 1¼ cups frosting in a pastry bag fitted with a ¼-inch plain or star tip. Cover the sides and top of the cake with the remaining frosting. Spread the remaining ½ cup preserves over the top, covering it evenly. Pipe frosting in a lattice pattern on top of the cake (7 diagonal lines in each direction). Gently press the chopped hazelnuts onto the sides. Pipe a line of frosting around the top edge where the frosting and nuts meet. Store in the refrigerator. Let stand for at least 2 hours at room temperature before serving.

Theresa S. Martin, Essex Junction, Vermont
Champlain Valley Fair and Exposition, Essex Junction, Vermont

Blue Ribbon Tip

IS WHITE CHOCOLATE REALLY CHOCOLATE?

Some people say that white chocolate is not real chocolate because it contains no cocoa solids. Good quality white chocolate, however, does contain cocoa butter and is truly delicious. When melted, it sets faster than dark chocolate, so you have to work fast. At room temperature, white chocolate is a little softer than dark. Note that because it contains milk solids, its shelf life is much shorter than that of dark chocolate.

White Cake with Coconut and Whipped Cream

12 servings

The fresh coconut in this recipe is so different and refreshing that it makes this cake a memorable one.

Cake
3 cups cake flour
1½ teaspoons baking powder
½ teaspoon baking soda
1 teaspoon salt
⅓ cup butter
⅓ cup shortening
1¾ cups sugar
½ teaspoon almond extract
½ teaspoon lemon extract
1 teaspoon vanilla
4 egg whites
1⅓ cups buttermilk

Filling
1 cup sour cream
1 cup confectioners' sugar
3 cups frozen or freshly grated
    coconut (about 1 coconut)

Whipped Cream
2 cups whipping cream, well
    chilled
5 tablespoons confectioners'
    sugar, sifted
1 teaspoon vanilla

sweetened coconut (optional)
maraschino cherry (optional)

To make the cake, preheat the oven to 375° F. Grease and flour 2 nine-inch round cake pans. Sift together the flour, baking powder, baking soda, and salt. Cream the butter and shortening. Add the sugar, creaming thoroughly. Stir in the almond extract, lemon extract, and vanilla. Add half the egg whites and beat vigorously until fluffy. Add the remaining egg whites and beat again. Add the dry ingredients and buttermilk alternately, stirring well. Pour into the prepared pans and bake for 23 to 25 minutes, or until a toothpick inserted in the center comes out clean. Cool in the pans on wire racks for 5 minutes. When barely cool, remove from the pans and split the layers in half with a thread or bread knife.

To make the filling, combine all the ingredients in a large bowl. Whisk until fluffy.

To make the whipped cream, combine all the ingredients in a chilled bowl and whip with a chilled beater until stiff peaks form.

Place one-quarter of the whipped cream on top of the first split layer, spreading evenly to a ½-inch thickness. Spoon one-quarter of the filling on top of the cream and spread it to the edges of the cake. Repeat for each split layer, stacking the layers as you go. After the cream and filling are spread on top of the cake, sprinkle with coconut and garnish with a maraschino cherry if desired. Keep cake chilled until serving time.

Annie Davis, Watauga, Tennessee
Appalachian Fair, Gray, Tennessee

Blue Ribbon Tip

CRACKING THE COCONUT

Fresh coconut adds a whole different flavor to your baking. To choose a good coconut, make sure that you can hear the liquid inside when you shake it. To open it, make two holes with a screwdriver and hammer and pour the liquid out. Using a hammer or the back side of a cleaver or heavy knife, hit the coconut repeatedly around its equator until it cracks open. Break the coconut into smaller pieces with a hammer. Remove the shell by slipping a knife between it and the meat and prying the shell off. Use a vegetable peeler to scrape off the brown skin. Cut the coconut into 1-inch pieces and grate by chopping in a food processor or blender. Frozen coconut is available in many Mexican and Latin American specialty stores. It defrosts quickly and is very easy to use.

Black Walnut Layer Cake

12 servings

This is a scrumptious and very memorable cake featuring the distinctive flavor of the American black walnut.

Cake
2 cups flour
1 teaspoon baking soda
¼ teaspoon salt
½ cup (1 stick) butter or
   margarine
½ cup shortening
2 cups sugar
5 eggs, separated
1 teaspoon vanilla
1 cup buttermilk
1½ cups chopped black walnuts

1 cup sweetened coconut
½ teaspoon cream of tartar

Frosting
½ cup (1 stick) butter or
   margarine
1 package (8 ounces) cream cheese
1 teaspoon vanilla
3½ cups confectioners' sugar

½ cup sweetened coconut
½ cup chopped black walnuts

To make the cake, preheat the oven to 350° F. Generously grease and flour 3 nine-inch round cake pans. In a medium-size bowl, sift together the flour, baking soda, and salt. In a large bowl, combine the butter, shortening, and sugar. Beat until smooth and well blended. Add the egg yolks and vanilla and beat well. Add the flour mixture gradually, alternating with the buttermilk, and beat until the batter is smooth. Stir in the walnuts and coconut.

Using clean beaters and a medium-size bowl, beat the egg whites and cream of tartar until stiff but moist peaks form. Gently fold into the batter. Divide the batter evenly between the prepared pans. Bake for 30 minutes, or until a toothpick inserted in the center comes out clean. Cool in the pans on wire racks for 10 minutes. Remove from the pans and cool completely on racks.

To make the frosting, in a medium-size bowl cream the butter, cream cheese, and vanilla until well blended. Beat in the confectioners' sugar and continue beating until the mixture is smooth and of spreading consistency. Frost the top of one layer and place another layer on it. Frost the top of this layer and place the third layer on it. Frost the sides and top of the cake.

Sprinkle coconut on top and carefully sprinkle black walnuts in a ring around the outside edge of the cake.

Nancy Johnson, Clever, Missouri
Ozark Empire Fair, Springfield, Missouri

Blue Ribbon Tip

THE ELUSIVE BLACK WALNUT

Most of us are used to English walnuts. The native American species is called the American black walnut and has a rich, distinctive flavor. You'll have to search to find them (some health food and specialty food stores carry them), but this blue ribbon winner will show them off to their best advantage. To order black walnuts by mail, write to Hammons Pantry, 105 Hammons Dr., Stockton, MO 65785, or call them at 1-800-872-6879. If you must, you may substitute English walnuts for American black walnuts.

Chocolate Coconut Cream Cake

10 to 12 servings

Renee Janas-Johnson has won the grand sweepstakes in the cake category with this recipe, and she also has won the General Mills Softasilk Flour Contest and the Nestlé Choco-Bake Challenge.

Cake
2 cups cake flour
2 cups sugar
1 teaspoon baking soda
1 teaspoon salt
½ teaspoon baking powder
¾ cup water
¾ cup buttermilk
½ cup shortening (do not use butter)
2 eggs
1 teaspoon coconut extract
4 envelopes (1 ounce each) premelted unsweetened chocolate

Filling
¼ cup (½ stick) butter, softened
¼ cup shortening
1 cup marshmallow cream
1½ teaspoons coconut extract
1¼ cups confectioners' sugar, sifted

Frosting
¼ cup milk
¼ cup (½ stick) butter
1 cup semisweet chocolate chips
1 teaspoon vanilla
2½ cups confectioners' sugar, sifted

toasted coconut (optional)

To make the cake, preheat the oven to 350° F. Grease and flour 2 nine-inch round aluminum cake pans (do not use nonstick pans). Place all the ingredients in a large mixer bowl. Blend for 30 seconds on low, scraping the bowl constantly. Beat for 3 minutes on high, scraping the bowl occasionally. Pour evenly into the prepared pans. Bake for 30 to 35 minutes, or until a toothpick inserted in the center comes out clean. (Do not overbake.) Cool in the pans on wire racks for 10 minutes. Remove from the pans and cool completely on racks.

To make the filling, cream the butter and shortening thoroughly. Add the marshmallow cream and coconut extract and beat well. Add the confectioners' sugar and beat until smooth. Spread half of the filling over one cake layer. Place the second cake layer on top and cover with the remaining filling.

To make the frosting, place the milk, butter, and chocolate chips in a saucepan over medium heat, stirring constantly until the chocolate and butter are melted. Remove from the heat and add the vanilla and confectioners' sugar. Mix until smooth. Frost the sides of the cake. Put the remaining frosting in a pastry bag fitted with a star tip and pipe around the top and bottom. If desired, sprinkle toasted coconut inside the piping on top.

Renee Janas-Johnson, Brooklyn Park, Minnesota
Minnesota State Fair, St. Paul, Minnesota

Pumpkin Cake

12 servings

Tammy Reiss is no stranger to blue ribbons, and this cake is a consistent winner. Our recipe tester rates it "absolutely delicious."

Cake
1½ cups vegetable oil
2 cups flour
2 cups sugar
1½ cups solid-pack pumpkin
4 eggs
2 teaspoons baking soda
3 teaspoons ground cinnamon
1 teaspoon vanilla

Frosting
1 package (8 ounces) cream cheese
¼ cup (½ stick) butter
2½ cups confectioners' sugar
2 teaspoons vanilla
1 cup nuts, chopped

To make the cake, preheat the oven to 350° F. Mix all the ingredients together until smooth. Pour into a greased 12-cup bundt pan and bake for 1½ hours, or until a toothpick inserted in the cake comes out clean. Cool in the pan on a wire rack for 10 to 15 minutes. Remove from the pan.

To make the frosting, beat the cream cheese and butter. Beat in the confectioners' sugar and vanilla. Stir in the nuts and spread on the cake while it is still slightly warm.

Tammy Reiss, Moore, Oklahoma
Oklahoma State Fair, Oklahoma City, Oklahoma

Chapter 5

Unfrosted Cakes

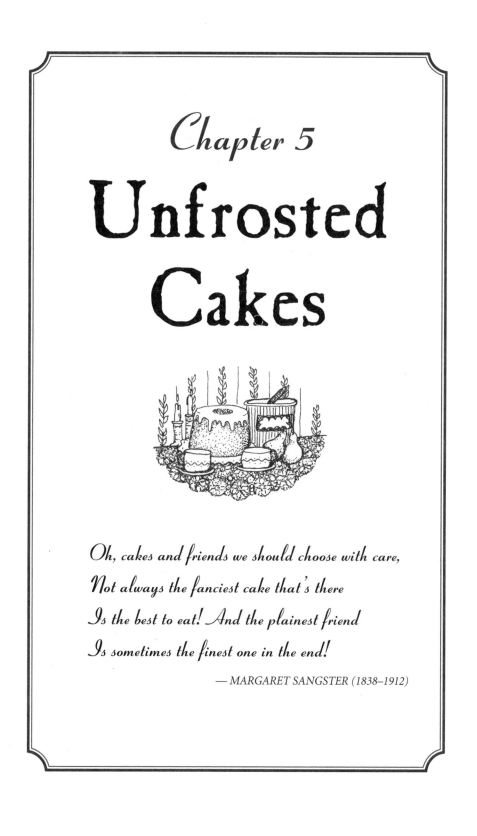

Oh, cakes and friends we should choose with care,
Not always the fanciest cake that's there
Is the best to eat! And the plainest friend
Is sometimes the finest one in the end!

— MARGARET SANGSTER (1838–1912)

Coconut Cake

12 servings

This recipe is a wonderful variation on a traditional pound cake. The buttery richness sets off the coconut to make a treat that will be long remembered. Quick to make, too! Our recipe tester notes that this is the cake her son keeps asking her to make again.

Cake
1 pound (4 sticks) butter, softened
2 cups sugar
2 cups flour, divided
6 eggs
2¼ cups (7 ounces) unsweetened
   coconut

1 teaspoon vanilla

Glaze
¼ cup water
½ cup sugar
¼ teaspoon almond extract

To make the cake, preheat the oven to 375° F. Butter and flour a 10-inch tube pan. Cream the butter and sugar. Add 1 cup of the flour. Beat in the eggs one at a time. Add the remaining 1 cup flour and beat. Add the coconut and vanilla and beat until well mixed. Pour into the prepared pan and bake for about 1¼ hours, or until a toothpick inserted in the cake comes out clean. Cool on a wire rack for about 10 minutes before removing from the pan.

To make the glaze, while the cake is still warm, combine the water, sugar, and almond extract. Pour slowly over the cake. Cool completely before serving.

Carrie O'Sullivan, Flemington, New Jersey
Flemington Agricultural Fair, Flemington, New Jersey

Blue Ribbon Tip

CREAM THE BUTTER
AND SUGAR THOROUGHLY

Many baking recipes start out with the instruction "cream the butter and sugar until light and fluffy." Many of us do this with only moderate energy – after all, everything gets all mixed together in the end, right? Not so. It turns out that this creaming operation incorporates precious bubbles of air into the fat. These bubbles will later be enlarged by the leavening agent (usually baking powder, baking soda, or both), but if the bubbles are not present, the baking powder or soda has nothing to work on, and the cake will not rise very high. For a successful cake, it is essential to cream the butter and sugar thoroughly. In the old days, a pastry chef had to have a very strong arm, but modern appliances make this job easy. You can leave a heavy-duty mixer to cream the butter and sugar while you assemble the other ingredients or grease the pans. It is not possible to do the job quite as well with a hand-held mixer. But whatever tools you use, taking time to cream the butter and sugar well will help your cake rise to impressive heights.

Orange Chiffon Cake

12 servings

Our recipe tester called this cake "A#1." It is light, delicious, and very hard to stop eating.

Cake
2¼ cups cake flour
1½ cups sugar, divided
1 teaspoon salt
1 teaspoon baking powder
½ cup vegetable oil
6 egg yolks
¼ cup water
½ cup freshly squeezed orange juice

zest of 1 orange
1 tablespoon vanilla
1 cup egg whites (about 8 eggs)

Glaze
⅔ cup confectioners' sugar, sifted
2 tablespoons freshly squeezed orange juice
2 teaspoons orange zest

To make the cake, preheat the oven to 325° F. Sift together the flour, ¾ cup of the sugar, salt, and baking powder. In a large bowl, beat the oil, egg yolks, water, orange juice, orange zest, and vanilla. Stir in the dry ingredients and blend well. With clean beaters, beat the egg whites in a large mixer bowl until fluffy. Gradually add the remaining ¾ cup sugar and beat until stiff and glossy but not dry. Stir one-third of the whites into the batter, then carefully fold in the remaining whites. Pour into an ungreased 10-inch tube pan and bake for 1 hour, or until the cake bounces back when touched. Immediately invert the pan over a bottle to hang. When completely cool, remove from the pan.

To make the glaze, stir together all the ingredients until smooth. Brush over the cake.

Robert Markey, Phoenix, Arizona
Arizona State Fair, Phoenix, Arizona

Cowboy Cobbler

24 servings

This recipe was developed by the cook's grandfather, who was a cowboy. He made it with wild peaches, cooking it in a Dutch oven buried in hot coals. The butter on the bottom is the secret to its melt-in-your-mouth goodness. Apples, pears, nectarines, or other fresh fruits that keep their texture, or even well-drained canned fruit, can be substituted for the peaches.

½ cup (1 stick) butter
1 cup flour
1 cup sugar
½ teaspoon salt
2 teaspoons baking powder

1 cup milk
2 teaspoons vanilla
2 to 3 cups peeled and sliced
 peaches

Preheat the oven to 350° F. Place the butter in a 13x9-inch glass baking dish and place in the oven until the butter is melted. (Or melt in the microwave and put in the oven to warm.) Combine the flour, sugar, salt, and baking powder in a medium-size bowl. Add the milk and vanilla and mix with a wooden spoon until well blended. Pour over the melted butter. Bake for about 15 minutes, or until the batter has risen. Arrange the peaches on top. Bake until a toothpick inserted in the top comes out clean, about 45 minutes. Serve warm either plain or with ice cream.

Susan Young, Castleton, Vermont
The Old Farmer's Almanac Recipe Contest, Dublin, New Hampshire

Blue Ribbon Tip

PEELING PEACHES

To peel peaches, bring a few quarts of water to a boil on the stove. Put the peaches in one or two at a time, remove with a slotted spoon and plunge into cold water. The peels will slide right off.

Buttermilk Poppy Seed Cake

12 to 14 servings

½ cup poppy seeds	½ cup brown sugar
1 cup buttermilk	4 eggs, separated
½ cup (1 stick) butter	2½ cups flour
½ cup shortening	1 teaspoon baking powder
½ teaspoon vanilla	1 teaspoon baking soda
1 cup granulated sugar	1 teaspoon salt

Preheat the oven to 350° F. Lightly grease a nonstick 12-cup bundt pan. Soak the poppy seeds in the buttermilk for 5 to 8 minutes. In a large bowl, cream the butter, shortening, and vanilla. Beat in the granulated sugar and brown sugar until light and fluffy. Add the egg yolks. Sift together the flour, baking powder, baking soda, and salt. Add to the sugar mixture alternately with the buttermilk, beating after each addition. Beat the egg whites until they are stiff but not dry. Fold half of them into the batter. Gently fold in the remaining whites. Pour into the prepared pan and bake until a toothpick inserted in the cake comes out clean, 35 to 45 minutes. Cool in the pan on a wire rack for 20 minutes, then turn out onto the rack to finish cooling.

Hilda Garey, St. Albans, Vermont
Vermont Dairy Festival, Enosburg Falls, Vermont

Perfect Pound Cake

12 to 16 servings

2 cups (4 sticks) unsalted butter,
   softened
3 cups sugar
6 eggs
4 cups flour, sifted

1 teaspoon baking powder
½ teaspoon salt
1 cup milk
1 teaspoon lemon extract

Preheat the oven to 300° F. Grease a 12-cup bundt pan. Cream the butter and sugar until light and fluffy. Add the eggs one at a time, beating well after each addition. Add the flour gradually. Beat in the baking powder, salt, milk, and lemon extract until smooth. Pour into the prepared pan. Bake for 1 hour 20 minutes, or until a toothpick inserted in the cake comes out clean. Cool in the pan on a wire rack for 10 minutes. Remove from the pan and cool completely on the rack.

Sue Thomas, Indianapolis, Indiana
Indiana State Fair, Indianapolis, Indiana

Pearadise Tart

8 to 10 servings

1 cup firmly packed brown sugar
¼ cup (½ stick) butter, softened
1 egg
½ teaspoon vanilla
¾ cup plus 1½ tablespoons
    cake flour
½ teaspoon baking powder
½ teaspoon salt

1⅓ cups peeled, cored, and finely
    chopped Bosc pears, divided
    (use firm, ripe pears)
¼ cup walnuts, chopped
⅓ to ½ cup raspberry preserves
1 or 2 Bosc pears, peeled, cored,
    and thinly sliced
½ teaspoon lemon juice
fresh mint sprig

Preheat the oven to 375° F. Grease and flour an 8-inch round baking pan. Line the pan with parchment or wax paper. Grease and flour the paper. In a large bowl, cream the brown sugar and butter until light and fluffy. Beat in the egg until smooth, then beat in the vanilla. Sift together the flour, baking powder, and salt. Stir into the batter. Mix in 1 cup of the chopped pears and the walnuts. Pour into the prepared pan and bake for 30 to 35 minutes, or until a toothpick inserted in the center comes out clean. Cool in the pan on a wire rack for 10 minutes. Remove from the pan. Carefully remove the wax paper and cool completely on the rack.

Place the tart on a serving plate. In a small bowl, stir together the preserves and remaining ⅓ cup chopped pears. Spoon over the tart, allowing a little to run over the sides. Arrange the pear slices in the center of the tart. Brush lightly with the lemon juice. Place the mint sprig in the center.

Ashlene Drake, Salem, Oregon
Oregon State Fair and Expo, Salem, Oregon

Plantation Pecan Cake

12 to 20 servings

The prunes in this recipe are its secret ingredient. They subtly improve the flavor while making the texture remarkably tender.

1 cup vegetable oil	½ teaspoon ground allspice
2 cups sugar	½ teaspoon ground cinnamon
3 eggs	1 teaspoon ground nutmeg
2 cups flour	1 cup buttermilk
1 teaspoon salt	1 cup chopped cooked prunes
1 teaspoon baking soda	4 cups coarsely chopped pecans

Preheat the oven to 350° F. Grease a 12-cup bundt pan. Beat the oil, sugar, and eggs until fluffy. Sift together the flour, salt, baking soda, allspice, cinnamon, and nutmeg. Add to the batter alternately with the buttermilk. Stir in the prunes and pecans. Pour into the prepared pan and bake for 1 hour, or until a toothpick inserted in the cake comes out clean. Cool in the pan for 20 to 30 minutes. Carefully remove from the pan and cool on a wire rack.

Emily James, Boyce, Louisiana
Louisiana Pecan Festival, Colfax, Louisiana

Blue Ribbon Tip

THE PLEASING PECAN

Pecans are unique to the Americas. Many people prefer them to walnuts for baking because they are less bitter. Pecans have the highest fat content of any nut, and this doubtless is one reason we love them so much. The fat in all nuts can cause them to become rancid, however, so any shelled nuts that you plan to store for more than a month should be kept in the freezer.

Cranberry and Pear Butter Crumb Cake

10 to 12 servings

Topping
¾ cup plus 1 tablespoon flour
⅓ cup firmly packed brown sugar
pinch of salt
¼ cup (½ stick) unsalted butter,
   melted and cooled

Cake
1 cup (2 sticks) unsalted butter
1 cup firmly packed brown sugar
4 eggs
1 teaspoon vanilla

1¾ cups white flour
½ cup whole-wheat flour
1½ teaspoons baking powder
½ teaspoon salt
1 cup fresh cranberries, coarsely
   chopped
1 firm, ripe pear, peeled, cored,
   and coarsely chopped
¼ cup granulated sugar
2 teaspoons lemon zest
2 teaspoons lemon juice

To make the topping, combine the flour, brown sugar, and salt in a bowl. Add the butter and cut into the dry ingredients to make damp crumbs. Set aside.

Preheat the oven to 350° F. Butter a 9-inch springform pan.

To make the cake, beat the butter and brown sugar on medium-high for 1 minute. Beat in the eggs one at a time, then beat in the vanilla. Sift the white flour, whole-wheat flour, baking powder, and salt into a separate bowl. Stir the dry ingredients into the creamed mixture in 2 stages, mixing just until the batter is smooth. In a separate bowl, combine the cranberries, pear, granulated sugar, lemon zest, and lemon juice. Fold a little more than half of the fruit mixture into the batter, then spread evenly in the pan. Spread the remaining fruit on top, leaving the edges of the batter un-covered. Scatter the crumb topping evenly over the fruit. Bake for 45 to 50 minutes, or until a toothpick inserted in the center comes out clean. Cool in the pan on a wire rack for 15 minutes, then carefully remove the sides of the pan. Slice and serve warm or at room temperature.

Ken Haedrich, Rumney, New Hampshire
Great New England Food Festival, Boston, Massachusetts

Blue Ribbon Tip

ZESTIER LEMON

Lemon zest is best made using a zester, a small, inexpensive tool with a little row of holes that remove only the outer, colored part of the rind. Lacking a zester, you can remove strips with a vegetable peeler and then chop them finely. Grated lemon rind often includes part of the pith of the lemon (the white part of the peel just under the yellow), and this can impart a bitter flavor to foods.

Pineapple Cheesecake

10 to 12 servings

Pineapple and cheese make a divine combination, as this unusual recipe demonstrates. Our recipe tester notes, "Yum, yum, yum; this was a personal favorite."

Crust
1½ cups graham cracker crumbs
3 tablespoons sugar
¼ cup (½ stick) butter, melted
¼ teaspoon ground cinnamon

Filling
2 cups cottage cheese
4 eggs
3 packages (8 ounces each) cream cheese

2 tablespoons flour
1 cup sugar
1¼ teaspoons vanilla
¼ teaspoon salt
2 cans (20 ounces each) crushed pineapple

Topping
2 cups sour cream
3 tablespoons sugar

To make the crust, preheat the oven to 300° F. Combine the graham cracker crumbs, sugar, butter, and cinnamon. Press into the bottom and 1½ inches up the sides of a 10-inch springform pan. Bake for 10 minutes. Maintain the oven temperature.

To make the filling, mix the cottage cheese and eggs in a blender. Beat the cream cheese, flour, sugar, vanilla, salt, and cottage cheese mixture until smooth. Drain the pineapple thoroughly. Fold the pineapple into the cream cheese mixture. Pour into the crust. Bake for 1½ hours. Turn the oven off and cool in the oven, with the door ajar, for 1 hour. Remove from the oven.

To make the topping, preheat the oven to 350° F. Combine the sour cream and sugar. Spread over the cheesecake and bake for 10 minutes. Cool slightly and refrigerate until serving time.

Signe Cole, Newport, Maine
Central Maine Egg Festival, Pittsfield, Maine

Chocolate Caramel-Pecan Cheesecake

8 to 10 servings

Crust
1 package chocolate wafers
½ cup chopped pecans
½ cup (1 stick) unsalted butter, melted

Filling
3 packages (8 ounces each) cream cheese
⅓ cup dark brown sugar
¼ cup dark corn syrup
2 tablespoons cornstarch
3 eggs
1 egg yolk
⅓ cup sour cream
1¼ teaspoons vanilla
1¾ cups milk chocolate chips
½ cup finely chopped pecans

Topping
¾ cup milk chocolate chips
¼ cup sour cream
1 tablespoon brown sugar
10 to 12 pecan halves

Caramel Sauce
10 or 11 vanilla caramels
2 tablespoons sour cream

Preheat the oven to 350° F. To make the crust, finely grind the chocolate wafers with the pecans. Stir in the butter and press into the bottom and up the sides of a 9-inch springform pan.

To make the filling, combine the cream cheese, brown sugar, corn syrup, and cornstarch and beat until smooth. Add the eggs and egg yolk one at a time, beating well after each addition. Stir in the sour cream and vanilla. Melt the chocolate chips and stir into the cream cheese mixture. Fold in the pecans and pour into the crust. Bake for 15 minutes. Turn the oven down to 200° F and bake for 1 hour 10 minutes, or until the center is no longer shiny. Turn the oven off and let the cake sit in the oven with the door closed for 1 hour. Refrigerate overnight.

To make the topping, melt the chocolate chips. Stir in the sour cream and brown sugar. Spread on top of the cheesecake and top with the pecan halves. Chill thoroughly.

To make the caramel sauce, melt the caramels and stir in the sour cream. Drizzle over the cake before serving.

Robin L. Warchol, Clinton Township, Michigan
Michigan State Fair, Detroit, Michigan

Angel Food Cake

12 to 16 servings

Even people who think they don't like cake usually like this one. We always make it when the accumulation of egg whites in the refrigerator gets unmanageable. It also makes a very welcome addition to any tea table.

12 egg whites   1 cup flour
¼ teaspoon salt   1½ teaspoons vanilla
1½ teaspoons cream of tartar
1½ cups granulated sugar   confectioners' sugar (optional)

Preheat the oven to 375° F. Beat the egg whites until foamy. Add the salt and cream of tartar and beat until soft peaks form. Add the granulated sugar 2 tablespoons at a time and beat until stiff and glossy. Carefully fold in the flour and vanilla. Pour into an ungreased 10-inch tube pan. Bake for 30 to 35 minutes, or until the cake bounces back when gently touched. Invert over a bottle and allow to hang until completely cool. Sprinkle with confectioners' sugar if desired.

Susan Smith, DeSoto, Texas
State Fair of Texas, Dallas, Texas

Blue Ribbon Tip

BEATING THE EGG WHITES INTO SHAPE

Cream of tartar is indispensable to angel food cake. It is often added to egg whites to stabilize them so that they will not lose their volume when they are folded into a batter. In the case of angel food cake, it also helps stabilize the air bubbles in the batter during the time it is in the oven, so the cake will hold its shape and not fall. Besides cream of tartar, another good thing for picture-perfect angel food cake is an old-fashioned tool that folds in egg whites or whipped cream extremely well. It has a small (2-inch-square), flat piece of wood with a hole in the middle attached to a handle. Another tool that works well looks like an oval fly swatter, with a much larger mesh. Either will do a good job of folding in egg whites with no loss of volume and no leftover pockets of batter or flour.

Banana Marble Pound Cake

10 to 12 servings

2½ cups sugar
½ cup shortening
½ cup (1 stick) butter, softened
4 eggs
2 medium-size ripe bananas
1 teaspoon vanilla
½ teaspoon lemon extract

3 cups cake flour
½ teaspoon baking soda
¾ cup plus ½ tablespoon
    buttermilk, divided
⅔ cup mini semisweet chocolate
    chips
2 tablespoons unsweetened cocoa

Preheat the oven to 325° F. Grease and flour a 10-inch tube pan. Cream the sugar, shortening, and butter until fluffy. Add the eggs one at a time, beating well after each addition. Add the bananas, vanilla, and lemon extract and beat well. Stir together the flour and baking soda and add to the batter alternately with ¾ cup of the buttermilk; beat well. Reserve ⅔ cup batter. Add the chocolate chips to the remaining batter and pour into the prepared pan. Add the cocoa and remaining ½ tablespoon buttermilk to the reserved batter. Drizzle onto the center of the batter in the pan and swirl through with a knife. Bake for 1¼ to 1½ hours, or until a toothpick inserted in the cake comes out clean. Cool in the pan on a wire rack for 10 minutes. Invert and cool completely on the rack.

Sally Crossan, Bear, Delaware
Delaware State Fair, Harrington, Delaware

Cherry Pudding Cake

8 servings

This is a great everyday dessert — who doesn't like cherries? — and it's easier and less expensive than pie.

Cake	Sauce
½ cup (1 stick) butter	water
1 cup sugar	reserved cherry juice
2 eggs	1 cup sugar
½ cup milk	1 tablespoon cornstarch
1½ cups flour	1 tablespoon butter
2 teaspoons baking powder	salt
½ teaspoon salt	ground nutmeg
½ teaspoon ground nutmeg	
1 can (16 ounces) pitted tart cherries, drained (juice reserved)	

To make the cake, preheat the oven to 350° F. Grease an 8-inch square baking pan. In a large bowl, use an electric mixer to cream the butter and sugar until light and fluffy. Add the eggs and milk and beat until well blended. Combine the flour, baking powder, salt, and nutmeg. Add to the batter and beat well. Gently stir in the cherries and pour into the prepared pan. Bake for 45 to 50 minutes, or until a toothpick inserted in the center comes out clean. Cool slightly in the pan on a wire rack.

To make the sauce, add enough water to the cherry juice to make 2 cups. Combine with the sugar and cornstarch in a small saucepan. Cook over high heat, stirring constantly, until the mixture thickens and bubbles. Turn the heat down and cook for 1 minute, stirring constantly. Remove from the heat and stir in the butter. Add salt and nutmeg to taste. Serve warm over the cake.

Mrs. Guy Hoenke, Traverse City, Michigan
National Cherry Festival, Traverse City, Michigan

Old-Fashioned Gingerbread

6 to 8 servings

½ cup (1 stick) butter or
  margarine
½ cup sugar
1 egg
1 cup molasses
2½ cups flour
1½ teaspoons baking powder

1 teaspoon ground cinnamon
2 teaspoons ground ginger
½ teaspoon ground cloves
½ teaspoon salt
1 cup hot water
whipped cream (optional)
confectioners' sugar (optional)

Preheat the oven to 350° F. Grease an 8- or 9-inch square pan. Cream the butter and sugar until light and fluffy. Beat in the egg and molasses. Sift together the flour, baking powder, cinnamon, ginger, cloves, and salt. Add to the batter alternately with the hot water. Pour into the prepared pan and bake for 35 minutes, or until a toothpick inserted in the center comes out clean. Serve warm with whipped cream or a dusting of confectioners' sugar if desired.

Karen Ritchie, Worthington, Ohio
Ohio State Fair, Columbus, Ohio

Chapter 6

Fruit Pies

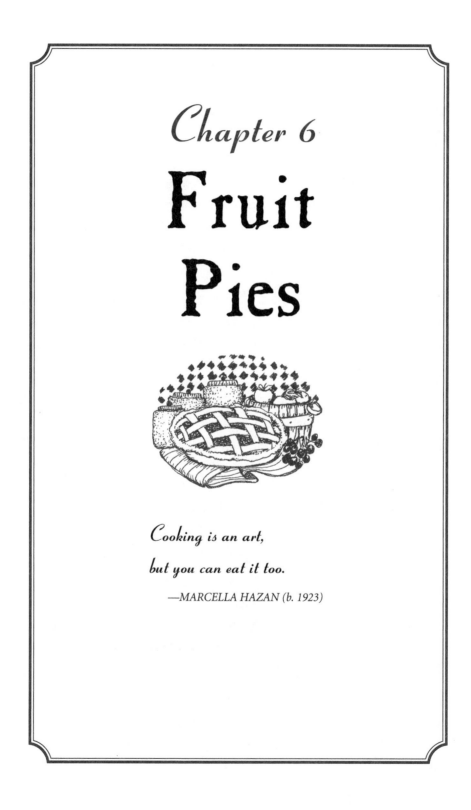

Cooking is an art,

but you can eat it too.

—MARCELLA HAZAN (b. 1923)

Blue Ribbon Tip

THE PERFECT COOKING APPLE

When a recipe calls for "tart cooking apples," what do you use? There is much debate on this question, and apple growers in Washington think quite differently than those in Michigan, who think differently than those in Vermont and upstate New York. A few varieties that seem to win praise from everyone are Gravenstein, Rhode Island Greening, and pippin, but it's hard to find these if you don't have a specialty orchard nearby. We recommend that you look for McIntosh or Cortland. Opinion is divided on Granny Smith and Golden Delicious, with some cooks claiming they make the best pies ever and others swearing they are tasteless and don't cook properly. Try them and come to your own conclusions. The most important factor is that the apples are fresh. Therefore, a variety that is ideal in early fall, such as McIntosh, might not be the best choice in winter, when you might want to consider Northern Spy instead.

In any case, the key to a delicious pie is to use the freshest apples, because storage tends to make apples mushy and bland.

A Great American Apple Pie

8 servings

Amy Fuqua always uses Winesap apples for this pie. She believes that only these apples keep a strong flavor after baking. Many of us cannot find Winesaps, so we tried making it with McIntoshes. Although it's probably not quite the same, it sure is good. Amy double-bakes her apples to fit in even more fruit. All the butter she uses to bake the apples keeps them from getting mushy.

Crust
2 cups flour
½ teaspoon salt
¾ cup cold lard
¼ cup (½ stick) cold butter
⅓ cup ice water (approximately)

Filling
12 Winesap apples
1 tablespoon lemon juice
⅓ cup granulated sugar
½ teaspoon ground cinnamon
⅛ teaspoon ground nutmeg
⅛ teaspoon ground cloves
6 tablespoons butter, melted
⅓ cup lightly packed brown sugar
1 heaping tablespoon cornstarch

To make the crust, combine the flour and salt. Cut in the lard and butter using a pastry blender or food processor. Add just enough ice water for the dough to form a ball. Roll out into 2 circles to fit a 9-inch pie plate, wrap in plastic wrap, and chill for a few hours or overnight.

To make the filling, preheat the oven to 375° F. Peel, core, and dice the apples. Add the lemon juice, sugar, cinnamon, nutmeg, cloves, and butter; mix well. Bake in a covered dish for 40 minutes. Drain the juice from the apples and reserve. Set aside. In a small saucepan, combine the brown sugar, cornstarch, and reserved apple juice. Cook over high heat, stirring constantly, until thick and bubbly. Pour over the apples and stir gently.

Preheat the oven to 450° F. Line a pie plate with one crust. Fill with the apple mixture. Cover with the other crust and crimp to seal. Prick the top crust to make steam vents. Bake for 15 minutes, then reduce the oven temperature to 350° F and bake for 35 minutes more, or until golden brown and bubbly. Cool on a wire rack.

Amy Fuqua, Boulder, Colorado
National Pie Championship, American Pie Council, Boulder, Colorado

Blueberry Streusel Pie

8 servings

Some people like this recipe even better than plain blueberry pie, and that's saying quite a lot. Try it for a change.

1 cup sour cream
¾ cup plus 2 tablespoons sugar
1 egg
5 tablespoons flour, divided
1 teaspoon vanilla
¼ teaspoon salt

2½ cups fresh or frozen
   blueberries
1 unbaked 9-inch pie shell
3 tablespoons butter
3 tablespoons pecans, chopped

Preheat the oven to 400° F. Beat the sour cream with ¾ cup of the sugar, egg, 2 tablespoons of the flour, vanilla, and salt for 5 minutes. Fold in the blueberries. Pour into the pie shell and bake for 25 minutes.

Meanwhile, combine the remaining 3 tablespoons flour and 2 tablespoons sugar. Cut in the butter. Stir in the pecans. Sprinkle on the pie and bake for 15 minutes more.

Loleta Dayton, Springfield, Missouri
Ozark Empire Fair, Springfield, Missouri

Blue Ribbon Tip

WILD BLUEBERRIES

Wild blueberries are a specialty of the barrens and mountaintops of Maine. They are much smaller and sweeter than their commercially grown cousins, and they are starting to become available in the frozen food section of many supermarkets. If you cannot find wild blueberries and wish to substitute commercial berries, you may need to increase the amount of sugar slightly.

Wild Blueberry Pie

8 servings

This recipe comes from Maine, where wild blueberries grow rampant. Tapioca makes an especially nice thickener for this and other fruit pies.

Crust
2 cups flour
½ teaspoon salt
¾ cup shortening
5 to 6 tablespoons cold water

Filling
⅔ cup sugar
3 tablespoons quick-cooking tapioca
1 teaspoon ground cinnamon
4 cups fresh or frozen wild blueberries
freshly squeezed lemon juice
1 tablespoon butter or margarine

Preheat the oven to 425° F.

To make the crust, sift together the flour and salt. Cut in the shortening using a pastry blender or food processor. Gradually add the water until the mixture pulls away from the sides of the bowl. Form into a ball and divide in half. Roll each half out into a circle big enough to line a 9-inch pie plate. Line the plate with one circle.

To make the filling, combine the sugar, tapioca, and cinnamon in a large bowl. Add the berries and stir to coat. Pour into the bottom crust. Drizzle with lemon juice and dot with the butter. Place the top crust over the filling, seal the edges, and flute. Pierce the top crust several times to allow steam to escape. Bake for 20 minutes. Reduce the oven temperature to 350° F and bake for 30 minutes more, or until the crust is golden. (Frozen berries may take 10 to 15 minutes longer. You may need to cover the edges with aluminum foil to prevent overbrowning.)

Sue Alimi, Fryeburg, Maine
Fryeburg Fair, Fryeburg, Maine

Delicious Rhubarb Pie

8 to 10 servings

Some people forget that there is more to rhubarb than just strawberry-rhubarb pie. This delicious variation combines rhubarb with orange for a sensational taste treat. You may substitute cherry or strawberry juice for the orange juice.

pastry for double-crust
   10-inch pie
4 cups rhubarb cut into
   ½-inch pieces
⅞ cup sugar
2 tablespoons quick-cooking
   tapioca

½ cup orange juice
1 tablespoon cornstarch
¼ teaspoon salt
1 egg, beaten
¼ teaspoon ground mace

Preheat the oven to 425° F. Line a pie plate with half the pastry. Place he rhubarb in the bottom crust. Stir together all the remaining ingredients and pour evenly over the rhubarb. Top with the other half of the pastry and seal the edges. Bake for 45 minutes, or until the rhubarb is tender.

Yolanda Bequeath, McDonald, Ohio
Canfield Fair, Canfield, Ohio

Blue Ribbon Tip

MACE AND NUTMEG

Mace and nutmeg are products of the same tree, native to the Moluccas (formerly known as the Spice Islands). That tree is now grown throughout Indonesia and in the Caribbean, particularly in Grenada. The fruit of the tree resembles a peach; its kernel is the nutmeg. Around this kernel grows a red, lacy covering, which is the mace. When the nutmeg is harvested, the fruit is discarded, the mace carefully separated, and the mace and nutmeg dried. Mace is usually somewhat more expensive than nutmeg, and its flavor is more subtle. It has long been appreciated in Europe, and more and more cooks in the United States are beginning to discover its delicate flavor.

Angie's Apple Crumb Pie

8 to 10 servings

Crust
1 cup flour
1 tablespoon sugar
¼ teaspoon salt
1 package (3 ounces) cream
  cheese, cubed
½ cup (1 stick) unsalted butter,
  cubed

Filling
⅔ cup sugar
½ teaspoon salt
½ teaspoon ground cinnamon
¼ teaspoon ground cloves

¼ teaspoon ground ginger
6 tart apples, peeled, cored, and
  thinly sliced
2 tablespoons orange juice
2 tablespoons lemon juice
2 tablespoons butter

Topping
½ cup brown sugar
¼ cup granulated sugar
¾ cup flour
½ cup (1 stick) butter, softened
½ cup freshly grated Parmesan
  cheese

To make the crust, in a large bowl combine the flour, sugar, and salt. With a pastry blender or two knives, cut in the cream cheese and butter until the mixture resembles coarse crumbs. Gently knead the dough into a ball, flatten slightly, cover, and refrigerate for 1 hour. Roll out the dough between 2 sheets of wax paper. Peel off the top paper and invert the crust into a 9-inch pie plate. Refrigerate for at least 1 hour before filling.

Preheat the oven to 350° F.

To make the filling, in a large bowl combine the sugar, salt, cinnamon, cloves, and ginger. Add the apples and sprinkle with the orange and lemon juices. Toss until evenly coated. Pour into the bottom crust and dot with the butter.

To make the topping, in a large bowl combine the brown sugar, granulated sugar, and flour. Work in the butter with your fingertips or a pastry blender until the mixture resembles coarse crumbs. Add the cheese and stir until mixed. Sprinkle over the filling and bake for 50 minutes to 1 hour, or until bubbly.

Angie H. Price, Pembroke, Virginia
The Old Farmer's Almanac Recipe Contest, Dublin, New Hampshire

Peach Pie

10 to 12 servings

This prizewinning pie is simple to make, showing that sometimes you can't beat the basics. Serve warm with whipped cream or ice cream.

pastry for double-crust 9-inch pie
¾ cup sugar
3 tablespoons flour
¼ teaspoon ground cinnamon

dash of salt
4 cups peeled and sliced peaches
 (about 7 or 8 peaches)
2 tablespoons butter or margarine

Preheat the oven to 400° F. Line a pie plate with half the pastry. Stir together the sugar, flour, cinnamon, and salt. Add the peaches and toss very gently to coat. Pour into the bottom crust and dot with the butter. Top with either a plain or lattice crust made from the other half of the pastry. Sprinkle with a little more sugar and cinnamon. Bake for 40 to 45 minutes, or until the filling is bubbly and the peaches are tender.

Mrs. Howard Cravens, Stonewall, Texas
Peach Jamboree and Rodeo, Stonewall, Texas

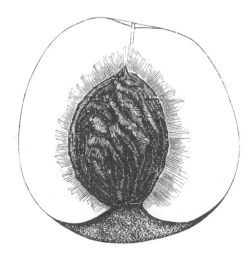

Downeast Burgundy Berry Pie

8 to 10 servings

"Downeast" has always been the name of the northeastern coast of Maine, because if you go downwind from Boston, that's where you'll end up. Both blueberries and cranberries grow wild on the starkly beautiful barrens there, and this pie celebrates both flavors.

pastry for double-crust 9-inch pie	2 cups fresh or frozen wild blueberries
1 cup sugar	1½ cups fresh or frozen cranberries
1 teaspoon ground nutmeg	2 tablespoons butter
3½ tablespoons cornstarch	
dash of salt	

Preheat the oven to 400° F. Line a pie plate with half the pastry. Stir together the sugar, nutmeg, cornstarch, and salt. Gently toss with the blueberries and cranberries. Pour into the bottom crust. Dot with the butter. Top with the other half of the pastry and seal. Cut a few slits in the top crust. Bake for 40 to 45 minutes, or until the crust is golden and the filling is bubbly.

Persis Jordan, Machias, Maine
Machias Wild Blueberry Festival, Machias, Maine

Pear-Almond Pie

8 to 10 servings

Crust
¾ cup almonds, toasted and
    chopped
1 baked 10-inch pie shell
½ cup almond paste

Filling
⅔ cup sugar
¼ cup cornstarch
¼ teaspoon salt
2 cups half-and-half
1 cup milk
3 egg yolks, slightly beaten

1 tablespoon butter
1½ teaspoons almond extract

Topping
1½ cups water
¾ cup sugar
1 teaspoon grated lemon rind
1 teaspoon vanilla
4 pears, peeled, cored, halved, and
    rubbed with lemon juice

1 cup apricot preserves
whipped cream (optional)
sliced almonds (optional)

To make the crust, sprinkle the almonds over the pie shell. Break up the almond paste into small bits and sprinkle it over the almonds.

To make the filling, mix the sugar, cornstarch, and salt in a saucepan. Add the half-and-half and milk and whisk to blend. Stirring constantly, bring to a boil over medium-low heat. Reduce the heat to low and cook, stirring constantly, for 1 minute. Gradually stir half of the hot milk mixture into the egg yolks and blend well. Return the mixture to the pan and boil for 2 minutes more, stirring constantly. Remove from the heat and add the butter and almond extract. Press plastic wrap down on top of the custard and cool.

To make the topping, combine the water, sugar, lemon rind, and vanilla in a saucepan and bring to a boil. Stir until the sugar is dissolved, then cover and simmer for 5 minutes. Place the pears cut side down in the syrup and simmer over low heat until they are tender when pierced with a fork, about 10 minutes. Carefully lift from the syrup and drain well. Cool.

Pour the cooled filling into the crust. Arrange the pears in a ring on top of the filling. Melt the apricot preserves over low heat. Press through a strainer to remove any bits of fruit. Lightly brush over the pear halves and filling. Decorate with whipped cream and sliced almonds if desired. Chill for several hours before serving.

Florence Neavoll, Salem, Oregon
Oregon State Fair and Expo, Salem, Oregon

All-American Apple Pie

8 to 10 servings

Is there any cook who does not aspire to making a really mouthwatering apple pie? It is sometimes tempting to search for the "secret ingredient" that will make your pie unique, but it usually turns out that the key to success is the quality of the apples themselves, with the quality of the pastry running a close second. Here is a recipe that we think approaches the ideal.

Crust
2 cups flour
1 teaspoon salt
⅔ cup cold unsalted butter
7 tablespoons water

Filling
7 cups peeled, cored, and thinly
    sliced tart cooking apples

2 tablespoons lemon juice
1 cup sugar
2 tablespoons flour
1 teaspoon ground cinnamon
⅛ teaspoon ground nutmeg
¼ teaspoon salt
2 tablespoons butter

Preheat the oven to 425° F.

To make the crust, sift together the flour and salt. Using a pastry blender, cut in the butter until the mixture is crumbly. Sprinkle on the water, stirring with a fork just until moistened. Form into a ball and divide in half. Roll each half out to a ⅛-inch thickness. Line a 9-inch pie plate with one half of the dough.

To make the filling, in a large bowl toss the apples with the lemon juice. Combine the sugar, flour, cinnamon, nutmeg, and salt. Add the apples and toss gently to coat. Pour into the bottom crust, mounding the apples high in the center. Dot with the butter.

Place the other half of the dough over the filling and fold it under the edge of the bottom crust. Press the edges together to seal, then crimp. Make at least 3 slits in the top to vent the steam. If desired, decorate with pastry scraps cut in the shape of apples. Bake for 45 to 50 minutes, or until the apples are fork-tender and the crust is golden brown. Cool on a wire rack.

Jean Thomas, Buchanan, Virginia
Salem Fair, Salem, Virginia

Schnappsy Peach Pie

10 servings

Because this crust calls for more shortening than usual, it is almost a short-bread — different and delicious.

Crust
3 cups flour
1 teaspoon salt
1½ cups butter or butter-flavored
  shortening
1 egg
1 tablespoon white vinegar
5 tablespoons cold water

Filling
¾ cup granulated sugar
½ cup packed brown sugar
2 tablespoons flour
½ teaspoon ground cinnamon
¼ teaspoon ground nutmeg
⅛ teaspoon ground cardamom
1½ cups peeled, cored, and sliced
  apples (about 3 apples)
1½ cups peeled and sliced
  peaches (about 3 peaches)
⅓ cup walnuts, chopped
1 teaspoon grated orange rind
½ teaspoon grated lemon rind
¼ cup peach schnapps
2 tablespoons butter

Preheat the oven to 375° F.

To make the crust, sift together the flour and salt. Add the butter or shortening and mix with a pastry blender. Beat the egg with the vinegar and water. Add to the dough and mix until it forms a ball. Divide in half and roll each half out into a circle large enough to line a 9-inch pie plate with a 1-inch overhang. Line the plate with one circle.

To make the filling, combine the granulated sugar, brown sugar, flour, cinnamon, nutmeg, and cardamom. Add the apples, peaches, walnuts, and grated orange and lemon rinds. Pour into the bottom crust. Pour the schnapps over the filling and dot with the butter. Cut out a design in the top crust if desired. Fold the crust gently in half and lift onto the filling. Unfold and crimp the edges together, trimming any excess. Bake for 12 minutes, then reduce the oven temperature to 350° F. Bake for 50 minutes more, or until the fruit is tender.

Darlene R. Lamp, Manning, Iowa
The Old Farmer's Almanac Recipe Contest, Dublin, New Hampshire

Cherry Pie

8 to 10 servings

David Oxley has made this blue ribbon winner dozens of times. His friends always request it for potluck suppers and special occasions, and even people who don't usually eat cherry pie say they like this one.

Crust
2 cups flour
1 teaspoon salt
⅔ cup shortening
5 to 7 tablespoons ice water

Filling
2 cans (16 ounces each) tart red
   cherries packed in water

1½ cups sugar, divided
⅓ cup cornstarch
dash of salt
1 tablespoon butter
4 drops almond extract

milk
sugar for sprinkling

Preheat the oven to 375° F.

To make the crust, stir together the flour and salt. Cut in the shortening with a pastry blender or food processor. Sprinkle the water over the mixture 1 tablespoon at a time, tossing with a fork after each addition. Add just enough water to moisten the dough. Form into a ball and divide in half. Roll each half out to fit a 9-inch pie plate. Line the plate with one half.

To make the filling, drain the cherries, reserving 1 cup of the juice. Combine ¾ cup of the sugar, cornstarch, and salt in a saucepan. Slowly add the reserved juice, stirring thoroughly to combine. Cook over medium heat, stirring constantly, until boiling. Continue cooking and stirring for 1 minute. Remove from the heat and mix in the butter and remaining ¾ cup sugar; stir to dissolve. Stir in the cherries and almond extract. Pour into the bottom crust. Cut the other half of the crust into ¾-inch-wide strips and weave into a lattice top. Crimp the edges. Brush the top with milk and sprinkle with sugar. Bake for 50 to 60 minutes, or until the top is nicely browned and the filling is thick and bubbly. Cool on a wire rack.

David Oxley, Seattle, Washington
Western Washington Fair, Puyallup, Washington

Chapter 7

Custard & Cream Pies

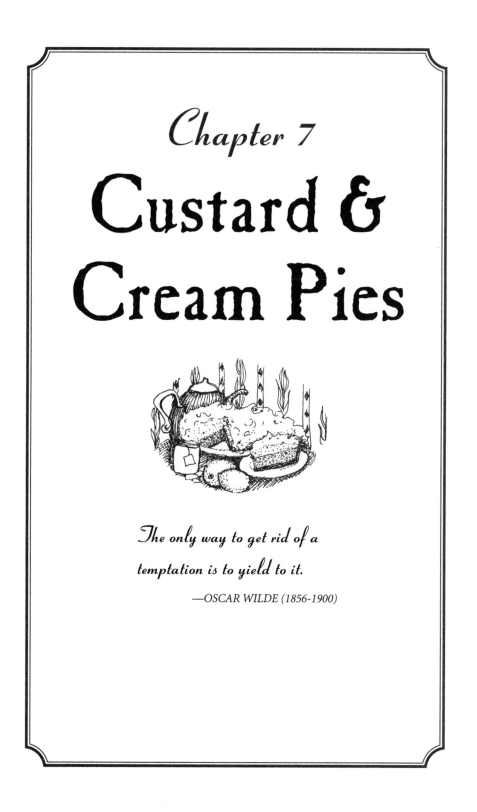

The only way to get rid of a temptation is to yield to it.

—OSCAR WILDE (1856-1900)

Coconut-Banana Cream Pie

8 servings

This recipe combines two unbeatable flavors for a dessert that leaves no question in your mind why it won both first place and an award of excellence.

Crust
3 cups sweetened coconut
7 tablespoons butter or margarine

Filling
¾ cup sugar
¼ cup flour
3 tablespoons cornstarch

¼ teaspoon salt
3 cups light cream
4 egg yolks, slightly beaten
2 teaspoons vanilla
2 large, firm bananas, sliced

1 cup whipped cream (optional)
sliced bananas (optional)

To make the crust, preheat the oven to 350° F. In a skillet, sauté the coconut in the butter until golden. Press all but 2 tablespoons into the bottom and up the sides of a greased 9-inch pie plate. Bake for 7 minutes.

To make the filling, combine the sugar, flour, cornstarch, and salt in a saucepan. Whisk in the cream and egg yolks and gradually bring to a boil over medium-low heat, stirring constantly. Boil for 2 minutes, stirring constantly. Remove from the heat and stir in the vanilla. Cool to room temperature. Place the 2 sliced bananas in the crust and cover with the custard. Chill until set, about 2 hours. Sprinkle with the 2 tablespoons coconut reserved from the crust. If desired, garnish with whipped cream and sliced bananas.

Melba Daniel, Hawkinsville, Georgia
Georgia National Fair, Perry, Georgia

Cranberry-Walnut Chess Pie

8 servings

The origin of the name "chess pie," traditionally associated with the South, is shrouded in mystery. One theory says that it is a variant of "Jes pie!" In any case, this version is an especially good one, as the tartness of the cranberries cuts the sweetness of this very rich treat.

1 cup fresh or frozen cranberries, chopped
1 ¼ cups sugar, divided
½ cup (1 stick) butter, softened
3 tablespoons flour
3 egg yolks

⅛ teaspoon salt
⅔ cup evaporated milk
1 teaspoon vanilla
½ cup walnuts, chopped
1 unbaked 8-inch pie shell

Preheat the oven to 375° F. Combine the cranberries and ¼ cup of the sugar and set aside. Beat the butter and the remaining 1 cup sugar until well blended. Add the flour, egg yolks, salt, and evaporated milk and beat. Stir in the cranberries, vanilla, and walnuts. Pour into the pie shell. Bake for 45 minutes, or until the center is still soft but almost set. Cool thoroughly on a wire rack.

Derolyn St. Louis, Freetown, Massachusetts
Cranberry Harvest Festival, Carver, Massachusetts

Pumpkin-Butterscotch Mousse Pie

8 servings

Butterscotch complements the flavor of pumpkin, and this recipe presents a delicious alternative to traditional pumpkin pie.

Crust
1¾ cups sweetened coconut
½ cup graham cracker crumbs
¼ cup (½ stick) butter or
  margarine, melted

1 package (12 ounces)
  butterscotch chips, divided

Filling
1 envelope unflavored gelatin

⅓ cup apple juice or water
1 package (3 ounces) cream
  cheese, softened
⅓ cup plus 1 tablespoon sugar,
  divided
1¼ cups solid-pack pumpkin
½ teaspoon pumpkin pie spice
¾ cup heavy cream

whipped cream (optional)

To make the crust, preheat the oven to 300° F. Combine the coconut and graham cracker crumbs in a medium-size bowl. Add the butter and mix until moistened. Press into the bottom and up the sides of a 9-inch pie plate. Bake for 20 to 25 minutes, or until golden brown.

Melt ½ cup of the butterscotch chips in a small, heavy saucepan over low heat. Spread thinly on the bottom of the crust. Chill.

To make the filling, soften the gelatin in the juice or water for 5 minutes. Heat gently over low heat until the gelatin is dissolved. Cool. Melt 1 cup butterscotch chips; cool slightly. In a large bowl, beat the cream cheese and ⅓ cup of the sugar until fluffy. Gradually beat in the gelatin mixture, melted butterscotch, pumpkin, and pumpkin pie spice. Chill until slightly thickened. Beat the cream with the remaining 1 tablespoon sugar until stiff peaks form. Fold into the pumpkin mixture. Spoon into the crust. Chill for at least 3 hours or overnight.

Before serving, melt the remaining ½ cup butterscotch chips. Thin as necessary with a little cream. Spoon into a small plastic bag. Snip a small corner from the bag and drizzle the butterscotch over the chilled pie. Add rosettes of whipped cream around the edge if desired.

Paula Rassi, Morton, Illinois
Morton Pumpkin Festival, Morton, Illinois

Pecan Custard Pie

10 servings

This is an interesting variation on traditional pecan pie. For people who like their pies light and fluffy, this slips right down.

1 envelope unflavored gelatin	1 teaspoon vanilla
½ teaspoon salt	1 cup pecans, chopped, divided
¾ cup dark brown sugar	½ cup granulated sugar
4 eggs, separated	1 baked 9-inch pie shell
4 tablespoons (½ stick) butter or	½ cup heavy cream, whipped
margarine, divided	
1 cup milk	

Combine the gelatin, salt, and brown sugar in the top of a double boiler. Heat slightly over hot, not boiling, water. Stir in the egg yolks, 2 tablespoons of the butter, and milk. Cook, stirring occasionally, until slightly thickened. Remove from the heat and add the vanilla. Cool, then chill in the refrigerator, stirring occasionally.

Sauté the pecans in the remaining 2 tablespoons butter, taking care not to burn the butter, until browned. Drain on paper towels. Beat the egg whites and granulated sugar until stiff peaks form. When the custard is thickened to the point where it mounds slightly when stirred with a spoon, fold in the egg whites and half the pecans. Pour into the pie shell and chill until firm to the touch. Top with the whipped cream and sprinkle with the remaining pecans.

Margaret Burlew, Houma, Louisiana
Louisiana Pecan Festival, Colfax, Louisiana

Chocolate-Rum Chiffon Pie

10 servings

Crust
1½ cups chocolate graham
   cracker crumbs
2 tablespoons sugar
pinch of salt
½ cup (1 stick) butter, melted

Filling
1 envelope unflavored gelatin
1 cup coffee, at room temperature

½ cup milk
2 squares (2 ounces) unsweetened
   chocolate, coarsely chopped
½ cup sugar, divided
¼ teaspoon salt
3 eggs, separated
2 tablespoons rum
1 teaspoon vanilla
1 cup whipping cream

To make the crust, preheat the oven to 325° F. Combine the graham cracker crumbs, sugar, and salt in a mixing bowl and toss together. Add the butter and stir vigorously until blended. Press the mixture into the bottom and up the sides of a 9-inch pie plate. Bake for 8 minutes. Cool completely.

To make the filling, sprinkle the gelatin over the coffee and let stand for a few minutes. In a saucepan, combine the milk and chocolate. Cook over low heat, stirring constantly, until the chocolate melts. Remove from the heat. Add ¼ cup of the sugar, salt, and egg yolks and whisk until well blended. Return to moderate heat and cook, stirring constantly, until the mixture thickens slightly and barely reaches a simmer, about 5 minutes. Do not boil. Add the softened gelatin and cook, stirring constantly, for about 1 minute more. Stir in the rum and vanilla. Pour into a bowl and chill, stirring occasionally, until it mounds when dropped from a spoon, about 1 hour.

Whip the cream until stiff. In another bowl, with clean beaters, beat the egg whites until soft peaks form. Fold the cream and egg whites into the chocolate mixture and pile into the crust. Chill for several hours before serving.

Kate Stewart Rovner, Plano, Texas
State Fair of Texas, Dallas, Texas

Lemon Sponge Pie

10 servings

Of this "Best of Show" pie, our recipe tester says enthusiastically, "I'll definitely be making this one again."

Crust
1 cup flour
½ teaspoon salt
⅓ cup shortening
2 tablespoons cold milk

Filling
3 tablespoons butter or
    margarine, softened

1¼ cups sugar
4 eggs, separated
3 tablespoons flour
dash of salt
1¼ cups milk
grated rind of 2 lemons
⅓ cup lemon juice

To make the crust, combine the flour and salt. Cut in the shortening until the mixture resembles coarse meal. Stir in the milk and form the dough into a ball. Roll out on a lightly floured surface to an 11-inch circle. Line a 9-inch pie plate with the dough and crimp the edges. Set aside.

To make the filling, preheat the oven to 375° F. In a large mixer bowl, cream the butter and sugar until fluffy. Beat in the egg yolks, flour, salt, milk, lemon rind, and lemon juice. In a small bowl, with clean beaters, beat the egg whites until stiff but not dry. Fold into the lemon mixture. Pour into the crust. Bake for 15 minutes. Reduce the oven temperature to 300° F and bake for 45 minutes more, or until the top is golden and a toothpick inserted in the center comes out clean. Cool on a wire rack.

Shirley M. Casity, New Springfield, Ohio
Canfield Fair, Canfield, Ohio

Coffee Cream Pie
with Chocolate Crust

8 to 12 servings

Crust
¼ cup (½ stick) unsalted butter
⅔ cup semisweet chocolate chips
1⅓ cups graham cracker crumbs

Filling
¼ cup instant coffee powder
2 tablespoons boiling water
1¼ cups milk

4 egg yolks
½ cup plus 2 tablespoons sugar, divided
3 tablespoons cornstarch
½ tablespoon unsalted butter
1 cup cold heavy cream
1 tablespoon semisweet chocolate chips, finely chopped

To make the crust, preheat the oven to 375° F. Generously butter a 9- or 10-inch pie plate. Melt the butter and chocolate chips in the top of a double boiler. Stir to mix well. In a bowl, combine with the graham cracker crumbs. Press firmly into the bottom and up the sides of the pie plate. Place in the freezer for 10 minutes. Remove from the freezer and bake for 8 minutes. Cool completely on a wire rack.

To make the filling, dissolve the coffee in the boiling water (this will be extra strong) and let sit for 15 minutes. Combine with the milk in a medium-size saucepan and heat until hot but not boiling. Meanwhile, in a large bowl beat the egg yolks, ½ cup of the sugar, and cornstarch until light and creamy. Slowly whisk in the hot milk until blended. Return to the saucepan and bring to a boil, whisking constantly. Boil for 1 minute. Pour into a bowl and stir in the butter. Place plastic wrap directly on the surface of the custard. Chill for about 1 hour. Whisk until smooth and light in color.

Beat the cream with the remaining 2 tablespoons sugar until fluffy and fully whipped. Fold about 1½ cups whipped cream into the custard. Spoon into the crust. Sprinkle with the finely chopped chocolate chips. Force the remaining whipped cream through a pastry tube or bag to decorate the pie. Chill for at least 4 hours. Let stand at room temperature for 15 minutes before serving.

Jeanne Lemlin, Great Barrington, Massachusetts
Great New England Food Festival, Boston, Massachusetts

Irish Potato Pie

8 to 10 servings

This recipe, with slight adjustments, was brought over "on the boat" by the cook's great-great-aunt shortly after a potato famine in the 1880s. When asked why she brought a potato pie (rather than a fruit pie) recipe with her, she'd answer, "Arragh, 'twas of no use in Ireland with nary a sound potato to be had there. May God bring them back." Of course, God did, and we celebrate that with the fine legacy of Aunt Bridget's delicate custard pie.

3 eggs
2 cups half-and-half or light
    cream
2 cups mashed potatoes (whipped
    smooth with no lumps)
1 cup sugar
1 teaspoon vanilla
¼ teaspoon salt
1 tablespoon Irish whiskey,
    brandy, or sherry (optional)
1 unbaked 10-inch deep-dish pie
    shell with high fluted edge
freshly grated nutmeg
toasted slivered almonds

Preheat the oven to 350° F. In a mixing bowl, beat the eggs slightly. Stir in the half-and-half or cream, potatoes, sugar, vanilla, salt, and liquor (if using). Beat well until smooth. Cover the fluted edge of the pie shell with aluminum foil to prevent overbrowning. Place on the center rack of the oven and carefully pour the filling into the shell. Sprinkle with nutmeg. Bake for 40 minutes. Remove the foil and bake for 15 to 18 minutes more, or until a knife inserted in the center comes out clean. Cool on a wire rack. Sprinkle the almonds around the outer edge and dust with additional nutmeg. Serve at room temperature; store in the refrigerator.

Mary Cummings, New Smyrna Beach, Florida
The Old Farmer's Almanac Recipe Contest, Dublin, New Hampshire

Sweet Potato–Pecan Pie

10 to 12 servings

This recipe won Raven Stocks first place in pies in the youth division. It tastes like a fancy pumpkin pie — perfect for a special holiday treat.

Filling

1 pound sweet potatoes (about 2 potatoes), cooked and peeled

¼ cup (½ stick) butter or margarine

1 can (14 ounces) sweetened condensed milk

1 teaspoon vanilla

1 teaspoon ground cinnamon

½ teaspoon ground nutmeg

½ teaspoon salt

2 eggs

1 unbaked 9-inch pie shell

Topping

1 egg

3 tablespoons light corn syrup

3 tablespoons light brown sugar

1 tablespoon butter or margarine, melted

½ tablespoon maple flavoring

1 cup pecans, chopped

Preheat the oven to 350° F.

To make the filling, in a large bowl beat the hot sweet potatoes and butter until smooth. Beat in all the remaining ingredients. Pour into the pie shell. Bake for 30 minutes. Maintain the oven temperature.

To make the topping, beat together all the ingredients. Pour over the filling. Bake for 20 minutes more. Cool completely on a wire rack.

Raven Stocks, Tabor City, North Carolina
North Carolina Yam Festival, Tabor City, North Carolina

Lemon Meringue Pie

10 to 12 servings

Crust
1 cup flour
¼ teaspoon salt
⅓ cup butter
3 to 4 tablespoons ice water

Filling
1½ cups sugar
⅓ cup plus 1 tablespoon
  cornstarch
¼ teaspoon salt
1½ cups water

3 egg yolks, slightly beaten
grated rind of 2 lemons
½ cup freshly squeezed lemon
  juice
3 tablespoons butter

Meringue
5 or 6 egg whites
¼ teaspoon cream of tartar
6 tablespoons sugar
½ teaspoon vanilla

To make the crust, preheat the oven to 425° F. Combine the flour and salt. Cut in the butter using a pastry blender or food processor. Gradually add water until the dough forms a ball. Roll out to fit a 9-inch pie plate. Line the pie plate with the dough. Crimp the edges and prick the bottom. Line the crust with aluminum foil and dried beans or pie weights. Bake for 10 minutes. Remove the foil and weights. Bake for 10 minutes more. Cool on a wire rack.

To make the filling, stir together the sugar, cornstarch, and salt in a medium-size saucepan. Whisk in the water and egg yolks. Bring to a boil over medium-low heat, stirring constantly. Boil for 1 minute. Remove from the heat and stir in the lemon rind, lemon juice, and butter. Pour into the crust.

To make the meringue, preheat the oven to 400° F. Beat the egg whites and cream of tartar until foamy. Gradually add the sugar and beat until stiff but not dry. Fold in the vanilla. Heap over the filling, being sure to bring the meringue well over the edges of the crust. Bake for about 10 minutes, or until lightly browned.

Kate Thomas, Fitzwilliam, New Hampshire
The Old Farmer's Almanac Recipe Contest, Dublin, New Hampshire

Date Delight

8 servings

2 cups graham cracker crumbs,
   divided
¼ cup (½ stick) butter, melted
¾ cup sugar, divided
2 slightly heaping tablespoons
   cornstarch
⅛ teaspoon salt

2 cups milk
2 eggs, separated
8 ounces dates, finely chopped
1 teaspoon vanilla
1 cup walnuts or pecans, chopped

whipped cream (optional)

Reserve ½ cup graham cracker crumbs. Combine the remaining crumbs and butter and press into the bottom and up the sides of a 9-inch glass pie plate. Mix together ½ cup of the sugar, cornstarch, and salt in a saucepan. Whisk in the milk and egg yolks. Bring to a boil over medium-low heat, stirring constantly. Boil for 1 minute. Cool. Pour into the crust and sprinkle the dates on top.

Preheat the oven to 350° F. Beat the egg whites until soft peaks form. Gradually add the remaining ¼ cup sugar and beat until stiff peaks form. Fold in the vanilla. Spread on top of the dates. Sprinkle with the nuts and reserved graham cracker crumbs. Bake for 30 to 40 minutes, or until golden brown. Chill overnight. Serve with whipped cream if desired.

Connie Harlow, Indio, California
National Date Festival, Indio, California

Chapter 8

Bars &
Brownies

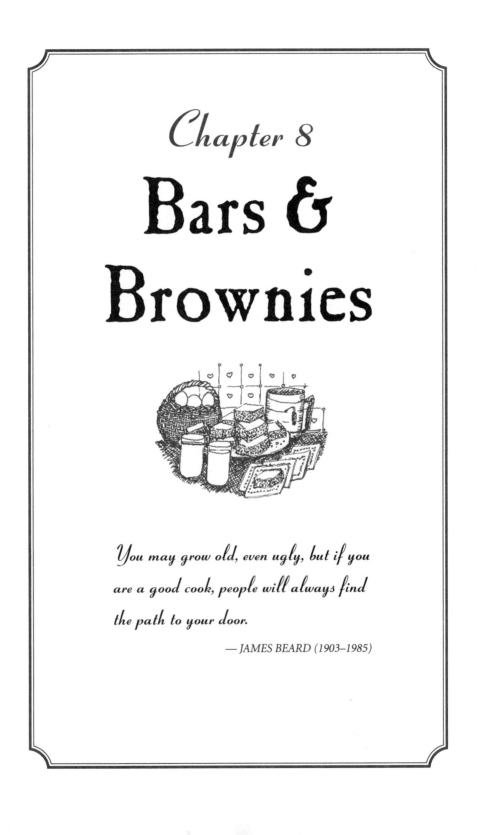

*You may grow old, even ugly, but if you
are a good cook, people will always find
the path to your door.*

— JAMES BEARD (1903–1985)

Pumpkin Cheesecake Bars

16 to 32 bars

These nice little treats are almost like individual pumpkin pies, but a bit creamier because of the cream cheese.

1 cup flour
⅓ cup loosely packed brown
   sugar
¼ cup (½ stick) butter, softened
½ cup pecans or walnuts, finely
   chopped
1 package (8 ounces) cream
   cheese

¾ cup granulated sugar
½ cup solid-pack pumpkin
2 eggs, slightly beaten
1 teaspoon vanilla
1½ teaspoons ground cinnamon
1 teaspoon ground allspice

Preheat the oven to 350° F. Combine the flour and brown sugar in a bowl. Cut in the butter to make a crumb mixture. Stir in the nuts. Set aside ¼ cup of this mixture. Press the remaining mixture into the bottom of an ungreased 8-inch square pan. Bake for 15 minutes. Cool slightly. Maintain the oven temperature.

Combine the cream cheese, granulated sugar, pumpkin, eggs, vanilla, cinnamon, and allspice in a bowl and blend until smooth. Pour over the baked crust. Sprinkle with the reserved crumbs. Bake for about 30 to 35 minutes. Cool, then cut into bars.

Deborah Taylor, Keene, New Hampshire
Great Gourd Bake-off, Keene, New Hampshire

Lemony Hazelnut Bars

20 bars

⅓ cup butter, softened
1 cup sugar, divided
1 cup plus 2 tablespoons flour,
    divided
½ cup ground toasted
    hazelnuts, divided
    (see tip on page 65)

2 eggs
½ teaspoon baking powder
2 teaspoons grated lemon rind
3 tablespoons freshly squeezed
    lemon juice
confectioners' sugar

Preheat the oven to 350° F. Beat the butter with an electric mixer for about 30 seconds. Add ¼ cup of the sugar and beat until combined. Beat in 1 cup of the flour and ¼ cup of the hazelnuts. Press into an ungreased 8-inch square pan. Bake for about 10 minutes, or until lightly browned. Maintain the oven temperature.

Combine the eggs, remaining ¾ cup sugar, remaining 2 tablespoons flour, baking powder, lemon rind, and lemon juice. Beat for 2 minutes, making sure the mixture is thoroughly combined. Pour over the hot crust and sprinkle the remaining ¼ cup hazelnuts on top. Bake for 20 minutes more, or until lightly browned. Cool completely, sprinkle with confectioners' sugar, and cut into bars.

Ellen West, South Deerfield, Massachusetts
Franklin County Fair, Greenfield, Massachusetts

Triple-Good Bars

4 dozen bars

2 cups raisins
1 can (14 ounces) sweetened
  condensed milk
1 tablespoon grated lemon rind
1 tablespoon lemon juice
1 cup (2 sticks) butter or
  margarine, softened
1⅓ cups firmly packed brown
  sugar

1½ teaspoons vanilla
1 cup flour
½ teaspoon baking soda
¼ teaspoon salt (optional)
2½ cups quick-cooking or
  old-fashioned oats
1½ cups chopped walnuts

Preheat the oven to 375° F. Grease a 13×9-inch baking pan.

In a medium-size saucepan, combine the raisins, condensed milk, lemon rind, and lemon juice. Cook over medium heat, stirring constantly, just until the mixture begins to bubble. Remove from the heat and cool slightly.

Beat the butter, brown sugar, and vanilla until fluffy. Add the flour, baking soda, salt (if using), oats, and walnuts. Blend until evenly mixed and crumbly. Press half of this mixture into the prepared pan. Spread the raisin mixture to within ½ inch of the edge. Sprinkle with the remaining oat mixture and pat lightly. Bake for 25 to 30 minutes, or until golden brown. Cool completely, then cut into 2×1-inch bars.

Carolyn Moreton, Flemington, New Jersey
Flemington Agricultural Fair, Flemington, New Jersey

Peanut Butter Bars

3 to 4 dozen bars

Peanut butter and chocolate are always a winning combination. These bars make an unbeatable lunch box treat.

Bars
½ cup (1 stick) butter or margarine, softened
½ cup crunchy peanut butter
½ cup loosely packed brown sugar
½ cup granulated sugar
1 egg
1 teaspoon vanilla
1 cup flour

½ cup quick-cooking or old-fashioned oats
1 teaspoon baking soda
¼ teaspoon salt
1 cup semisweet chocolate chips

Icing
½ cup confectioners' sugar
2 tablespoons creamy peanut butter
2 tablespoons milk

To make the bars, preheat the oven to 350° F. Grease a 13×9-inch baking pan. In a mixing bowl, combine the butter, peanut butter, brown sugar, and granulated sugar. Add the egg and vanilla and mix well. In another bowl, combine the flour, oats, baking soda, and salt. Stir into the peanut butter mixture. Spread in the prepared pan. Sprinkle with the chocolate chips. Bake for 20 to 25 minutes, or until lightly browned. Cool for 10 minutes.

To make the icing, combine all the ingredients and drizzle over the uncut bars. Cool completely before cutting.

Sharon Fish, Morrisville, Missouri
Ozark Empire Fair, Springfield, Missouri

Decadent Brownies

1 dozen brownies

Brownies
15 ounces fine European
  semisweet chocolate
¾ cup (1½ sticks) unsalted
  butter
¾ cup confectioners' sugar
2 tablespoons flour
4 eggs, separated
1 teaspoon vanilla
¾ cup sour cream

Glaze
¼ cup (½ stick) unsalted butter
4 ounces fine European semisweet
  chocolate
1½ cups confectioners' sugar
3 tablespoons boiling water or
  strong coffee
2 teaspoons vanilla

To make the brownies, preheat the oven to 375° F. Lightly grease a 9-inch square glass baking dish. Melt the chocolate and butter in a large saucepan. Whisk in the confectioners' sugar and flour and remove from the heat. Add the egg yolks one at a time, beating well after each addition. Stir in the vanilla. Beat the egg whites in a separate bowl until stiff, then fold into the chocolate mixture. Remove 1 cup of this mixture and blend with the sour cream; set aside. Pour the chocolate-egg mixture into the prepared pan. Top with the chocolate–sour cream mixture and swirl with a knife. Bake for 30 minutes. Cool completely.

To make the glaze, melt the butter and chocolate together. Remove from the heat and beat in the confectioners' sugar, water or coffee, and vanilla. Spread over the cooled brownies.

Jill Anderson, Perry, Georgia
Georgia National Fair, Perry, Georgia

Apricot-Almond Bars

4 dozen bars

This recipe makes a very fancy looking bar, suitable for holidays and the most elegant occasions.

Topping
1½ cups sugar
3 cups sliced almonds
4 egg whites (2 yolks reserved for crust)
2 tablespoons flour
½ teaspoon ground cinnamon
¼ teaspoon freshly grated nutmeg

Crust
2½ cups flour
½ cup sugar

1 cup (2 sticks) butter
2 egg yolks

Apricot Glaze
½ cup apricot preserves
1 tablespoon water

Chocolate Glaze
3 squares (3 ounces) semisweet chocolate
1 square (1 ounce) unsweetened chocolate

To make the topping, combine all the ingredients in the top of a double boiler. Cook, stirring occasionally, until the mixture reaches 110° F on a candy thermometer. Set aside.

To make the crust, preheat the oven to 350° F. Line a 15×10-inch jellyroll pan with aluminum foil. Combine the flour and sugar. Cut in the butter. Add the egg yolks and mix well. Press into the prepared pan. Bake for 15 minutes. Spread the topping over the crust and bake for 20 minutes more.

To make the apricot glaze, melt the apricot preserves with the water in a small saucepan. Brush over the topping immediately after the bars come out of the oven. Cool, then cut into 2-inch squares.

To make the chocolate glaze, melt the semisweet and unsweetened chocolate in the top of a double boiler. Drizzle on the bars. Allow to set.

Carolyn Rosen, Nashville, Tennessee
The Old Farmer's Almanac Recipe Contest, Dublin, New Hampshire

Caramel Rocky Road Bars

2 dozen bars

When Kimberly Roland was 13, she entered this recipe in the junior division of cookies and won "Best of Show."

Crust
1 cup flour
¾ cup quick-cooking or
   old-fashioned oats
½ cup sugar
½ cup (1 stick) butter, softened
½ teaspoon baking soda

¼ teaspoon salt
¼ cup salted peanuts, chopped

Filling
½ cup caramel ice cream topping
½ cup salted peanuts
1½ cups miniature marshmallows
½ cup milk chocolate chips

To make the crust, preheat the oven to 350° F. Grease and flour a 9-inch square baking pan. In a small mixer bowl, combine the flour, oats, sugar, butter, baking soda, and salt. Beat on low, scraping the bowl often, until the mixture is crumbly, about 1 to 2 minutes. Stir in the peanuts. Reserve ¾ cup of this mixture. Press the remaining mixture into the prepared pan. Bake for 12 to 17 minutes, or until lightly browned. Maintain the oven temperature.

To make the filling, spread the caramel topping over the hot crust. Sprinkle the peanuts, marshmallows, and chocolate chips over the top. Sprinkle on the reserved crumb mixture. Bake for 20 to 25 minutes, or until lightly browned. Cover and refrigerate for 1 to 2 hours, or until firm. Cut into bars with a hot knife.

Kimberly Roland, Forney, Texas
State Fair of Texas, Dallas, Texas

Yam-Oatmeal Squares

2 dozen squares

Crust
2 cups flour
1 cup brown sugar
1 cup (2 sticks) butter or
    margarine
1 cup quick-cooking oats

Filling
3 cups mashed sweet potatoes
    (about 2 large sweet potatoes)
1 teaspoon ground cinnamon
½ teaspoon ground nutmeg

1 teaspoon vanilla
1 cup evaporated milk
1 cup sugar
2 eggs
½ teaspoon salt

Topping
1 cup pecans, chopped
¼ cup (½ stick) butter or
    margarine
1 cup brown sugar

To make the crust, preheat the oven to 350° F. Combine the flour and brown sugar. Cut in the butter using a pastry blender or food processor. Stir in the oats. Press into an ungreased 13×9-inch baking pan. Bake for 15 minutes. Maintain the oven temperature.

To make the filling, combine all the ingredients. Pour over the crust. Bake for 20 minutes. Maintain the oven temperature.

To make the topping, combine all the ingredients. Sprinkle over the filling. Bake for 15 to 20 minutes, or until set. Cool, then cut into squares.

Suzette Leonard, Tabor City, North Carolina
North Carolina Yam Festival, Tabor City, North Carolina

The World's Best Brownies

4 dozen brownies

6 squares (6 ounces) unsweetened
   chocolate
1 cup (2 sticks) butter or
   margarine
6 eggs
3 cups sugar

3 tablespoons vanilla
¾ cup milk
2 cups flour
1½ teaspoons salt
1½ cups walnuts, chopped

Preheat the oven to 350° F. Grease and flour a 15×10-inch jellyroll pan. Melt the chocolate and butter in the top of a double boiler. Cool slightly. Beat the eggs until very thick, about 5 minutes. Gradually add the sugar and continue beating. Add the chocolate mixture and continue beating. Mix in the vanilla and milk and beat until smooth. Combine the flour and salt and add to the batter in fourths, beating well after each addition. Stir in the walnuts. Pour into the prepared pan and bake for 25 to 35 minutes, or until a toothpick inserted in the center comes out clean. Cool completely, then cut into bars.

Susan A. Silvashy, Laredo, Texas
Canfield Fair, Canfield, Ohio

Cherry-Filled White Chocolate Bars

20 bars

½ cup (1 stick) unsalted butter
1 package (12 ounces) white
    chocolate chips, divided
2 eggs
½ cup sugar
1 cup flour

½ teaspoon salt
½ teaspoon almond extract
½ cup sweetened coconut
½ cup cherry preserves
¼ cup sliced almonds

Preheat the oven to 325° F. Grease and flour an 8-inch square baking pan. Melt the butter in a small saucepan over low heat. Remove from the heat and add 1 cup of the white chocolate chips. Do not stir.

In a large bowl, beat the eggs until foamy. Add the sugar gradually, then stir in the chocolate mixture. Add the flour, salt, and almond extract. Mix just until blended. Spread half the mixture in the prepared pan. Bake for 15 to 20 minutes, or until light golden brown.

Meanwhile, add the remaining white chocolate chips and coconut to the remaining batter. Melt the cherry preserves over low heat. When the crust is ready, spread with the preserves and gently spoon the batter on top, spreading it to the edges. Sprinkle with the almonds. Bake for 20 to 25 minutes, or until set and light brown. Cool completely, then cut into bars.

Jackie de Matteis-O'Brien, Powell, Ohio
Ohio State Fair, Columbus, Ohio

Cream Cheese Swirl Brownies

9 large or 16 small brownies

Batter
4 squares (4 ounces) unsweetened
  chocolate
½ cup (1 stick) butter
1¼ cups sugar
½ teaspoon vanilla
3 eggs
¾ cup flour

Filling
1 package (8 ounces) cream cheese
1½ teaspoons flour
5 tablespoons sugar
1 egg
¼ teaspoon vanilla

Preheat the oven to 350° F. Grease an 8-inch square cake pan.

To make the batter, melt the chocolate and butter over low heat. Cool for 5 minutes. With an electric mixer, beat together the chocolate mixture, sugar, and vanilla. Beat in the eggs one at a time. Blend in the flour. Set aside.

To make the filling, beat together the cream cheese, flour, sugar, egg, and vanilla.

Spread about two-thirds of the batter in the bottom of the pan. Gently spread the filling over the batter. Spoon the remaining batter over the filling. Bake for 50 minutes. Cool in the pan, then cut into squares.

Mary Michelli, Leesburg, Georgia
Georgia National Fair, Perry, Georgia

Chapter 9
Cookies

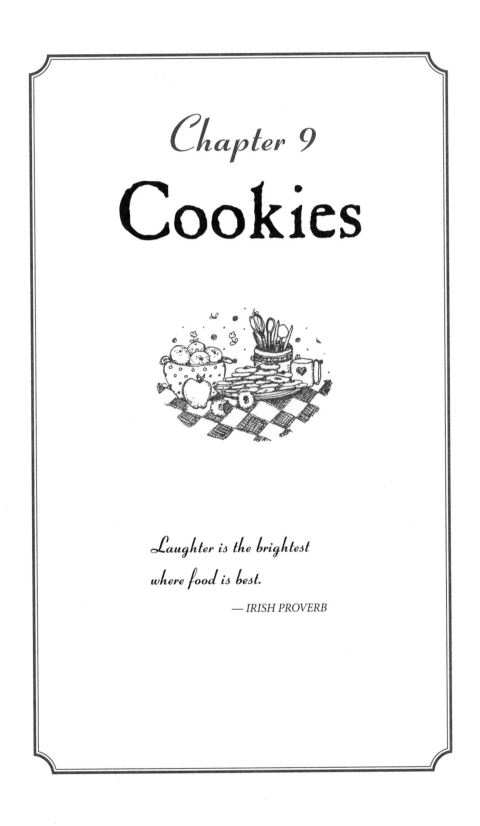

*Laughter is the brightest
where food is best.*

— *IRISH PROVERB*

Cranberry-Coconut Cookies with Toffee

18 cookies

It's really hard to eat just one of these yummy little treats, which look just as nice as they taste.

Crusts
½ cup (1 stick) butter
1 package (3 ounces) cream
   cheese, softened
1 cup flour

Filling
1 tablespoon butter, softened
3 tablespoons brown sugar

1 tablespoon milk
½ cup sweetened coconut
½ cup fresh or frozen cranberries,
   coarsely chopped
½ cup crushed chocolate-coated
   English toffee bars
   (two 1.4-ounce bars)

To make the crusts, preheat the oven to 350° F. Beat the butter and cream cheese. Stir in the flour. (This also works well in a food processor.) Cover and chill for about 1 hour, or until easy to handle. Shape into 1-inch balls. Press into the bottom and up the sides of 1¾-inch muffin cups (mini muffins). Bake for 10 minutes.

To make the filling, cream the butter and brown sugar. Add the milk and stir until well mixed. Stir in the coconut, cranberries, and crushed toffee bars. Fill the crusts with the cranberry mixture. Bake for 10 minutes more. Let cool in the pan for at least 10 minutes before removing.

Ann Marie Briand, New Bedford, Massachusetts
Cranberry Harvest Festival, Carver, Massachusetts

Empire Biscuits

20 cookies

These "biscuits" won first place in the Scottish Faire contest, and it is no wonder: the cook is from Scotland and treasurer of the Scottish Society of Iowa. She says that "everyone in Scotland makes this cookie." They are perfect for a formal tea but will be appreciated just as much in your child's lunch box.

2¼ cups flour
½ cup sugar
1 cup (2 sticks) butter, softened

raspberry preserves
confectioners' sugar

Preheat the oven to 325° F. Mix together the flour and sugar. Add the butter, working the dough together to form a ball. (This can be done in a food processor.) Turn out onto a lightly floured surface and roll out to a ⅛-inch thickness. Cut into 2-inch rounds. Place on ungreased cookie sheets and bake for 10 to 12 minutes. Cool on wire racks. When cool, sandwich 2 cookies together with raspberry preserves and sprinkle with confectioners' sugar.

Ann McWilliam, Melbourne, Iowa
Iowa State Fair, Des Moines, Iowa

Triple-Peanut Cookies

50 cookies

Peanut butter aficionados, take note! There's no shortage of real peanut flavor in these cute cookies.

½ cup granulated sugar
½ cup firmly packed brown sugar
½ cup shortening
¾ cup chunky peanut butter,
   divided
2 tablespoons light corn syrup
1 tablespoon milk

½ teaspoon vanilla
1½ cups flour
½ teaspoon baking soda
¼ teaspoon salt
½ cup roasted peanuts, chopped

In a large bowl, cream the granulated sugar, brown sugar, shortening, and ½ cup of the peanut butter with an electric mixer. Blend in the corn syrup, milk, and vanilla. In a separate bowl, sift together the flour, baking soda, and salt. Add to the creamed mixture, mixing thoroughly. Shape into a 1½-inch roll approximately 18 inches long. Wrap in plastic wrap and chill for at least 2 hours.

Preheat the oven to 350° F. Carefully cut the dough into ¼-inch slices. Place on ungreased cookie sheets and spread each cookie with a little of the reserved peanut butter. Crimp the edges with a fork and sprinkle the top with roasted peanuts. Bake for 12 to 14 minutes, or until lightly browned. (Do not overbake.) Cool on wire racks.

Shelly Ann Britton, Rochester, New Hampshire
Sandwich Fair, Center Sandwich, New Hampshire

Chocolate-Orange Delights

6 dozen cookies

The hint of orange adds just the right touch to these chocolaty goodies.

Cookies
3 squares (3 ounces) unsweetened
   chocolate
¾ cup (1½ sticks) butter
1 cup firmly packed brown sugar
1 cup granulated sugar
½ cup sour cream
2 eggs
2 teaspoons grated orange rind
2 cups flour
1 teaspoon baking soda

½ teaspoon salt
1 cup walnuts or pecans, chopped
1 package (12 ounces) semisweet
   chocolate chips

Glaze
3 squares (3 ounces) semisweet
   chocolate
1 teaspoon orange extract
4 tablespoons (½ stick) butter
candy sprinkles (optional)

To make the cookies, preheat the oven to 375° F. Melt the unsweetened chocolate and cool. Cream the butter, brown sugar, and granulated sugar until very light. Add the sour cream, eggs, orange rind, and melted chocolate; beat well. Stir in the flour, baking soda, and salt. Add the nuts and chocolate chips. Drop by rounded teaspoonfuls onto lightly greased cookie sheets. Bake for 12 to 15 minutes. Cool on wire racks.

To make the glaze, melt the chocolate with the orange extract in a small, heavy saucepan over low heat. Add the butter 1 tablespoon at a time. Stir until smooth. Spread on the cookies. If desired, decorate with candy sprinkles before the glaze hardens.

Frances E. Callahan, Chester, Vermont
The Old Farmer's Almanac Recipe Contest, Dublin, New Hampshire

Apple-Toffee Cookies

4 dozen cookies

For all those who love candied apples, these cookies combine caramel and apple in a form much easier to pack in a lunch box.

½ cup (1 stick) butter	2 teaspoons cream of tartar
½ cup shortening	1 teaspoon baking soda
1½ cups sugar	¾ teaspoon salt
2 eggs	1 package (8 ounces) almond
2¾ cups flour	brickle chips
2 teaspoons ground cinnamon	1 cup dried apples, diced

Preheat the oven to 400° F. Beat the butter, shortening, sugar, and eggs together until thoroughly mixed. Sift together the flour, cinnamon, cream of tartar, baking soda, and salt. Stir into the butter mixture until well combined. Add the almond brickle chips and dried apples; mix well. Spoon the mixture by teaspoonfuls onto ungreased cookie sheets. Bake for 8 to 10 minutes, or until lightly browned. (Do not overbake. The cookies will not be set in the middle.) Cool on wire racks.

Joy White, Noblesville, Indiana
Indiana State Fair, Indianapolis, Indiana

Blue Ribbon Tip

CHOPPING DRIED FRUIT

Dried fruit such as apples is very easy to chop using a meat grinder. Use the coarse blade and just run the fruit through. A food processor does not work well because the fruit can stick to the blade and become mushy.

Chocolate Peppermint Creams

3 dozen cookies

Consider these the cookie version of a peppermint patty. Our recipe tester notes, "My mother, who loves chocolate and peppermint, kept sneaking off to have another one of these. I was quite surprised, but this cookie seemed to bring out the five-year-old in her."

Cookies
3 cups flour
1¼ teaspoons baking soda
½ teaspoon salt
¾ cup (1½ sticks) butter
1½ cups firmly packed brown
   sugar
2 tablespoons water
1 package (12 ounces) semisweet
   chocolate chips
2 eggs

Peppermint Cream
3 cups confectioners' sugar
⅓ cup butter, softened
¼ teaspoon peppermint extract
   (or to taste)
¼ cup milk

To make the cookies, preheat the oven to 350° F. Sift together the flour, baking soda, and salt. In a large saucepan over low heat, melt the butter with the brown sugar and water. Add the chocolate chips and stir to melt. Remove from the heat, cool slightly, and beat in the eggs. Add the flour mixture and mix well. Drop by heaping teaspoonfuls onto greased cookie sheets and bake for 8 to 10 minutes. Cool on wire racks.

To make the peppermint cream, blend all the ingredients with a mixer until smooth. Sandwich pairs of cookies together with 1 teaspoon peppermint cream. Cookies taste best a few days after baking and freeze beautifully.

Roselie A. Aiello, Mount Shasta, California
The Old Farmer's Almanac Recipe Contest, Dublin, New Hampshire

Sima's Yummy Rugelach

2 dozen cookies

Sima Firine's mother brought this recipe from Russia when the family was smuggled out of the country in 1922. Sima was 13 at the time, and in the years between arriving in America and last year, when she won a blue ribbon for her rugelach, she figures she has made this recipe several hundred times. The name means "little horns," and that's just what they look like. The cream cheese makes for a delicious pastry.

½ cup (1 stick) unsalted butter, softened
1 package (8 ounces) cream cheese, softened

1 cup flour
½ cup walnuts, finely chopped
¼ cup sugar
½ teaspoon ground cinnamon

Cream the butter and cream cheese. Add the flour and mix well. (This can be done in a food processor.) Divide the dough in half and flatten. Wrap each half in wax paper and refrigerate overnight.

Preheat the oven to 350° F. Stir the walnuts, sugar, and cinnamon together in a small bowl. Roll out each half of the dough into an 8-inch circle. Sprinkle each with half the nut mixture. Cut each into 12 pie-shaped pieces. Starting at the wide end of each piece, roll it up toward the point. Place on a greased cookie sheet and bake for 20 minutes.

Sima Firine, Poughkeepsie, New York
Dutchess County Fair, Rhinebeck, New York

Molasses Cookies

5 dozen cookies

1½ cups shortening
2 cups sugar
½ cup light molasses
2 eggs
4 cups flour
4 teaspoons baking soda

1 teaspoon salt
1 teaspoon ground cloves
1 teaspoon ground ginger
2 heaping teaspoons ground
  cinnamon
sugar for rolling

Preheat the oven to 375° F. Cream the shortening and sugar. Add the molasses and eggs and beat. Add the flour, baking soda, salt, cloves, ginger, and cinnamon. Beat until well blended. Chill for 10 minutes. Roll into 1-inch balls. Roll in sugar, covering the balls completely. Bake on ungreased cookie sheets for 8 to 10 minutes. Cool on wire racks.

Kathy Mintun, San Francisco, California
California Exposition and State Fair, Sacramento, California

Blue Ribbon Tip

CINNAMON

Cinnamon is one of the most flavorful and best-known spices in the world. It is cultivated in Indonesia, China, Vietnam, and Sri Lanka (formerly Ceylon). Korintje Cassia cinnamon grows wild on the southern coast of Sumatra and is preferred by many bakers for its smooth flavor with less bite. Chinese cinnamon is stronger and spicier and has only recently become available outside China. Vietnamese cinnamon is the strongest cinnamon and is extremely sweet and flavorful. Ceylonese cinnamon, also known as true cinnamon, is unfamiliar to most Americans. It is not as strong as the other types, but it is preferred in England and Mexico.

German Hazelnut Cookies

5 dozen cookies

These are an authentic Old World Christmas treat, but we recommend that you don't save them just for Christmas!

3 cups flour
3 cups (6 sticks) ice-cold unsalted
    butter
3 cups confectioners' sugar
3½ cups ground hazelnuts or
    walnuts, divided

3 eggs, well beaten
juice and grated rind of 1 lemon
1 egg beaten with 1 tablespoon
    water

Measure the flour into a large bowl and cut in the butter. (This can be done in batches in a food processor.) Stir in the confectioners' sugar and 3 cups of the nuts. Add the eggs and lemon juice and rind. Cover tightly with plastic wrap and chill thoroughly, at least 2 hours.

Preheat the oven to 350° F. Working with a small amount of dough at a time (keep the rest of the dough refrigerated), roll out to a ¼-inch thickness on a floured surface. Cut with cookie cutters and transfer to greased cookie sheets. (The dough also may be dropped by teaspoonfuls. The cookies will flatten into brown-edged wafers as they bake.) Brush gently with the egg-water mixture and sprinkle with the remaining hazelnuts. Bake until golden, 10 to 15 minutes.

Mrs. Betty P. Race, Euclid, Ohio
The Old Farmer's Almanac Recipe Contest, Dublin, New Hampshire

Triple-Treat Peanut Butter Chocolate Chip Cookies

4 to 5 dozen cookies

These cookies make an ideal lunch box treat. Chocolate chips, oats, and peanut butter in one delicious cookie: who says you can't have it all?

1½ cups old-fashioned oats, divided

2 cups flour

1 teaspoon baking powder

1 teaspoon baking soda

1 teaspoon salt

1 cup (2 sticks) unsalted butter, softened

1 cup granulated sugar

1 cup firmly packed light brown sugar

1 tablespoon vanilla

¾ cup creamy peanut butter

2 eggs

1 package (12 ounces) semisweet chocolate chips

Reese's Pieces

Grind 1 cup of the oats in a blender or food processor until fine. In a large bowl, stir together the ground oats, remaining ½ cup whole oats, flour, baking powder, baking soda, and salt. In another bowl, cream the butter, granulated sugar, and brown sugar until light and fluffy. Beat in the vanilla and peanut butter. Beat in the eggs one at a time. Gradually add the oatmeal mixture and mix well. Stir in the chocolate chips. Chill for at least 2 hours (up to 1 week).

Preheat the oven to 325° F. Roll the dough into balls about 1 to 2 inches in diameter. Press a Reese's Piece on top of each one and place on an ungreased cookie sheet. Bake for 11 to 14 minutes. The cookies will be just barely set. Cool on wire racks.

Robin L. Warchol, Clinton Township, Michigan
Michigan State Fair, Detroit, Michigan

Raspberry-Orange Mazurkas

32 pastries

The mazurka is a traditional Polish dance. These heirloom Polish goodies are just as pretty and have the same exotic appeal as the spirited dance.

Crust
1 cup (2 sticks) unsalted butter, softened
1½ cups flour
1¼ cups confectioners' sugar
½ teaspoon salt
6 egg yolks

2 teaspoons orange extract
1 cup pecans, finely chopped

Topping
1 cup raspberry preserves
2 tablespoons orange liqueur
1 tablespoon grated orange rind

To make the crust, preheat the oven to 325° F. Grease and flour 2 nine- or ten-inch round cake pans. Cream the butter until light. Combine the flour, confectioners' sugar, and salt. Add to the butter alternately with the egg yolks. Add the orange extract and beat until smooth. Fold in the pecans. Pat into the prepared pans and bake for 35 to 40 minutes, or until golden. Cool on wire racks.

To make the topping, heat all the ingredients in a small saucepan. Strain the warm topping through a fine sieve. Using a serrated knife, cut each mazurka into 16 wedges, place on a serving tray, and glaze with the topping.

Kathy Lee, Valley Center, California
The Old Farmer's Almanac Recipe Contest, Dublin, New Hampshire

White Chip Chocolate Cookies

5 dozen cookies

Here are some chocolate chip cookies in reverse — white chocolate chips in a dark chocolate cookie.

1 cup (2 sticks) butter
¾ cup granulated sugar
⅔ cup brown sugar
2 eggs
1 teaspoon vanilla
2¼ cups flour

¾ cup unsweetened cocoa
1 teaspoon baking soda
½ teaspoon salt
1 package (12 ounces) white
     chocolate chips

Preheat the oven to 350° F. Beat the butter, granulated sugar, and brown sugar until fluffy. Beat in the eggs and vanilla. Sift together the flour, cocoa, baking soda, and salt. Beat into the batter until well mixed. Stir in the white chocolate chips. Drop by tablespoonfuls onto ungreased cookie sheets. Bake for 9 to 11 minutes. (Do not overbake.) Remove from the sheets immediately and cool on wire racks.

Jennifer Davis, Wellington, Kansas
Kansas Wheat Festival, Wellington, Kansas

Grandma's Best Butter Cookies

4 dozen cookies

This truly versatile recipe works just as well whether you make cookie-cutter cookies, cookies molded in a cookie press, refrigerator cookies, or just plain drop cookies. And no one can eat just one! Every cook needs this recipe in his or her repertoire.

1 cup (2 sticks) butter, softened	2¼ cups flour
¾ cup sugar	¼ teaspoon salt
2 egg yolks	
1 teaspoon vanilla, or	
1½ teaspoons almond extract	

Cream the butter and sugar until light and fluffy. Add the egg yolks and vanilla or almond extract and beat well. Sift the flour and salt into the batter and beat until well mixed.

To make drop cookies, preheat the oven to 350° F. Drop unchilled dough by teaspoonfuls onto cookie sheets lined with parchment paper (or ungreased). Bake for about 10 minutes, or until just barely brown at the edges. Cool on wire racks.

To make rolled (refrigerator) cookies, shape the dough into 2 rolls, each 1½ inches in diameter. Wrap in wax paper and chill for at least 1 hour. Preheat the oven to 350° F. If you wish, roll the dough in colored sugar, chocolate sprinkles, or rainbow sprinkles. Cut each roll into ½-inch slices, place on cookie sheets lined with parchment paper, and bake for 10 minutes. (Do not brown.) Cool on wire racks and store in an airtight container.

To make cookie-cutter cookies, chill the dough. Preheat the oven to 350° F. Roll out the dough between floured wax paper to a ½-inch thickness. Cut with cookie cutters (small ones work best). Place on parchment-lined cookie sheets and bake for 10 minutes. Cool on wire racks and decorate if desired. Sandwich cookies may be made by sticking two cookies together with preserves or almond filling.

To make molded cookies, preheat the oven to 350° F. Put the unchilled dough in a pastry bag with a big star tip or in a cookie press fitted with a design plate. Drop the cookies onto parchment-lined cookie sheets and bake for 10 minutes. Cool on wire racks. (Our recipe tester notes, "The molded cookies worked about the most easily in the cookie press of any recipe I have tried.")

Mary Ann Saint, Plymouth, Michigan
Michigan State Fair, Detroit, Michigan

Blue Ribbon Tip

DON'T DISCARD THOSE EGG WHITES!
Egg whites can be stored in the refrigerator or freezer. Keep an airtight container in the refrigerator for them. When a recipe calls for yolks, simply save the leftover whites in this container, where they will keep quite well for at least a month. When enough have accumulated, you can make an angel food cake. In the meantime, there are always enough to provide a few extra for a recipe like this one or to add to a meringue for a pie, making it extra high.

Orange Citrus Cookies

2 dozen cookies

Cookies
½ cup (1 stick) butter
1 cup sugar
1 egg
½ cup sour milk, or ½ cup milk
   plus ½ teaspoon lemon juice
3 cups flour
½ teaspoon baking soda
1 teaspoon baking powder

1 teaspoon orange extract
2 teaspoons grated orange rind
⅓ cup orange juice

Icing
3 tablespoons butter, softened
½ to 1 cup confectioners' sugar
1 drop red food coloring
1 drop yellow food coloring

To make the cookies, preheat the oven to 375° F. Cream the butter and sugar. Add the egg and beat well. Stir in the milk. Combine the flour, baking soda, and baking powder and add to the sugar mixture. Add the orange extract, orange rind, and orange juice and mix well. Drop by large spoonfuls on lightly greased cookie sheets. Bake for 10 to 12 minutes, or until just barely browned. Cool on wire racks.

To make the icing, cream the butter. Add enough confectioners' sugar to make the icing of spreading consistency. Add the red and yellow food coloring, then spread on the cooled cookies.

Jan Herrmann-Beach, Mesa, Arizona
Arizona State Fair, Phoenix, Arizona

Appendix

List of Fairs, Festivals & Bake-offs

Please contact organizers at the addresses and telephone numbers below for dates of fairs and guidelines for submitting entries. Also, please verify the cost of cookbooks and shipping fees before placing orders.

ALABAMA

National Peanut Festival
1691 Ross Clark Circle, SE
Dothan, AL 36301
(334) 793-4323
For a brochure of winning recipes, send a self-addressed, stamped envelope to the address above.

ARIZONA

Arizona State Fair
P.O. Box 6728
Phoenix, AZ 85005
(602) 252-6771
The cookbook *Arizona State Fair Blue Ribbon Recipes* is available for $10 plus $2.50 shipping.

CALIFORNIA

National Date Festival
Fairgrounds Office
46-350 Arabia Street
Indio, CA 92201
(619) 863-8247
For a brochure with date recipes, write to California Dates, P.O. Box 1736, Indio, CA 92201.

California Exposition and State Fair
P.O. Box 15649
Sacramento, CA 95852
(916) 263-3000

COLORADO

National Pie Championship
American Pie Council
P.O. Box 18793
Boulder, CO 80308
(303) 402-0702

Colorado State Fair
State Fairgrounds
Pueblo, CO 81004
1-800-444-FAIR or (719) 566-0530

DELAWARE

Delaware State Fair
P.O. Box 28
Harrington, DE 19952
(302) 398-3269

GEORGIA

Georgia National Fair
P.O. Box 1367
Perry, GA 31069
(912) 987-3247

ILLINOIS

Morton Pumpkin Festival
Morton Chamber of Commerce
415 W. Jefferson Street
Morton, IL 61550
(309) 263-2491

INDIANA

Indiana State Fair
1202 E. 38th Street
Indianapolis, IN 46205
(317) 927-7500

IOWA

Iowa State Fair
400 E. 14th Street
Des Moines, IA 50318-0198
(515) 262-3111

KANSAS

Kansas Wheat Festival
Wellington Area
  Chamber of Commerce
207 S. Washington Street
Wellington, KS 67152
(316) 326-7466

LOUISIANA

Louisiana Pecan Festival
P.O. Box 78
Colfax, LA 71417
(318) 627-5196

MAINE

Fryeburg Fair
P.O. Box 78
Fryeburg, ME 04037
(207) 935-3268

Machias Wild Blueberry Festival
Centre Street Congregational Church
P.O. Box 265
Machias, ME 04654
(207) 255-4402 or (207) 255-6665

Central Maine Egg Festival
P.O. Box 82
Pittsfield, ME 04967
(207) 487-3136

MASSACHUSETTS

YANKEE Magazine's Great New
  England Food Festival
33 Union Street
Boston, MA 02108
The festival which operated from 1986
to 1991, was a way of celebrating New
England cooks and manufacturers of
food products.

Cranberry Harvest Festival
P.O. Box 983
Carver, MA 02330
Cape Cod Cranberry Growers'
  Association
P.O. Box 730
E. Wareham, MA 02538
(508) 295-4895
  The Cape Cod Cranberry Growers'
Association has a store by the Cape
Cod Canal that is devoted exclusively
to cranberries, with gift baskets avail-
able for shipping. For information, call
(508) 759-8783.

Franklin County Fair
P.O. Box 564
Greenfield, MA 01302
(413) 774-4282

Shelburne Grange Fair
Fellowship Hall
Little Mohawk Road
Shelburne, MA 01370
(413) 625-9924

MICHIGAN

Michigan State Fair
Exposition Center
1120 W. State Fair
Detroit, MI 48203
(313) 369-8250

National Cherry Festival
P.O. Box 141
Traverse City, MI 49685
(616) 947-4230
  The festival sells the *Taste of Cherries Recipe Book* for $5 (includes shipping) and will give sources for cherry products of all kinds.

MINNESOTA

Minnesota State Fair
1265 Snelling Avenue North
St. Paul, MN 55108-3099
(612) 642-2200

MISSOURI

Ozark Empire Fair
P.O. Box 630
Springfield, MO 65801
(417) 833-2660
  The 60th Anniversary Cookbook is available for $11 (includes shipping).

NEW HAMPSHIRE

Sandwich Fair
P.O. Box 161
Center Sandwich, NH 03227
(603) 284-7062

The Old Farmer's Almanac Recipe
  Contest
Dublin, NH
P.O. Box 520
Dublin, NH 03444
(603) 563-8111
Each year, the Almanac announces a contest that features recipes with a specific ingredient (chicken, apples, or eggs, for example). Cash prizes are awarded for the best original recipes submitted.

Great Gourd Bake-off
Pumpkin Festival
Center Stage Cheshire County
95 Main Street
Keene, NH 03431
(603) 358-5344

NEW JERSEY

Flemington Agricultural Fair
P.O. Box 293
Flemington, NJ 08822
(908) 782-2413

NEW YORK

Dutchess County Fair
P.O. Box 389
Rhinebeck, NY 12572
(914) 876-4001

NORTH CAROLINA

North Carolina Yam Festival
P.O. Box 841
Tabor City, NC 28463
  The cookbook *Recipes from North Carolina Yam Festival* is available for $5 plus shipping.

OHIO

Canfield Fair
P.O. Box 250
Canfield, OH 44406
(216) 533-4107
  The *Canfield Fair Cookbook* is available for $8 plus $3 shipping and handling.

Ohio State Fair
717 E. 17th Avenue
Columbus, OH 43211
(614) 644-4040
The cookbook *Flavors of the Fair* is available for $14.95 plus $3 shipping.

OKLAHOMA

Oklahoma State Fair
P.O. Box 74943
Oklahoma City, OK 73147
(405) 948-6700

OREGON

Oregon State Fair and Expo
2330 17th Street NE
Salem, OR 97310
(503) 378-3247

Springfield Filbert Festival
Springfield Chamber of Commerce
101 S. A Street
Springfield, OR 97477
(541) 746-1651

RHODE ISLAND

Washington County Fair
Box 78, Richmond Townhouse Road
Carolina, RI 02812
(401) 782-8139

TENNESSEE

Appalachian Fair
Appalachian Fair Association, Inc.
P.O. Box 8218
Gray, TN 37615
(423) 477-3211

TEXAS

State Fair of Texas
P.O. Box 150009
Dallas, TX 75315
(214) 421-8716

The *State Fair of Texas Cookbook*, with 300 prizewinning recipes, is available for $20 (includes shipping) from Creative Arts, State Fair of Texas.

Peach Jamboree and Rodeo
Stonewall Chamber of Commerce
P.O. Box 1
Stonewall, TX 78671
(830) 644-2735

VERMONT

Vermont Dairy Festival
Attn: Noel Blouin
Enosburg Falls, VT 05450
(802) 933-4636

Champlain Valley Fair and Exposition
P.O. Box 209
Essex Junction, VT 05453
(802) 878-5545

VIRGINIA

Salem Fair
Salem Civic Center Complex
P.O. Box 886
Salem, VA 24153
(540) 375-3004

WASHINGTON

Western Washington Fair
P.O. Box 430
Puyallup, WA 98371
(206) 845-1771

WISCONSIN

Wisconsin State Fair
P.O. Box 14990
8100 W. Greenfield Avenue
West Allis, WI 53214
(414) 266-7000

Index